JN441164

Nielbock-Yoon Jaewon

DARAKWON

한국어를 열심히 공부했지만 실제로 대화를 하거나 드라마를 보다 보면 어딘가 따라가기 어렵다고 느낀 적이 있을 것입니다. 그 이유는 문법이나 새로운 어휘가 부족해서가 아니라 사람들이 어떻게 말을 시작하고, 이어 가고, 정리하는지 그 흐름에 익숙하지 않기 때문입니다. 이 책은 한국어 학습자들이 한국인의 말 습관과 대화 흐름을 이해하고 익히는 데 초점을 맞추었습니다.

100 Korean Speech Patterns에서는 한국 드라마 속 대사를 바탕으로 한국인이 일상 대화에서 자주 사용하는 말 습관을 '표현'과 '문형' 파트로 나누어 제시했습니다. 드라마는 허구의 이야기이지만 그 안에서 인물들의 말투와 대화 방식은 실제 언어 사용을 충실하게 담아냅니다. 따라서 장면 속 맥락을 따라가며 표현을 익히는 과정은 문법적인 설명만으로는 이해하기 어려운 언어의 감각을 자연스럽게 길러 줄 것입니다.

각 단원은 드라마 장면을 보여 주는 삽화와 대사를 통해 표현 및 문형이 사용되는 맥락을 먼저 파악한 후, 이어지는 간단한 퀴즈를 통해 표현의 의미와 쓰임을 스스로 생각해 보도록 하였습니다. 이후에는 표현이나 문형의 의미와 기능을 자세히 설명하고, 대화문을 통해 실제 사용 예시를 확인할 수 있도록 했습니다. 그리고 QR코드를 통해 음원을 들어 보면서 억양과 어감까지 한결 생생하게 익힐 수 있을 것입니다.

이 책의 집필에는 독일 보훔대학교에서 한국어를 배우는 학생들과 긴밀히 소통하며 현장의 언어 감각을 전해 준 류선희 선생님이 함께해 주셨습니다. 또한 책의 전체 구성과 편집 과정에서 한 문장 한 문장을 공들여 다듬고 세심하게 조언해 주신 다락원 한국어출판부 편집진께도 깊은 감사를 드립니다. 이분들의 노력 덕분에 스크린에서 튀어나온 듯한 살아있는 말들을 지금처럼 엮어낼 수 있었습니다.

이 책은 회화 능력을 빠르게 습득하는 것보다는 한국어로 말하는 상황 자체에 익숙해지는 것을 목표로 하고 있습니다. 따라서 학습 내용을 한 번 읽고 넘어가지 않고 여러 번 보고 듣고 말해 보며 표현이 자연스럽게 떠오를 때까지 시간을 들이기를 권합니다. 나중에 한국 드라마를 보다가 책에서 다룬 표현이 귀에 들어오거나, 한국어로 말을 하면서 배운 표현을 자연스럽게 사용하게 되면 공부에 자신감을 가지게 될 것입니다.

윤재원

Preface

Even if you have studied Korean diligently, you may have found that it still feels difficult to keep up when you try to have real conversations or watch Korean dramas. This is not because you lack grammar knowledge or vocabulary, but because you are not yet familiar with the flow of how people start a conversation, carry it forward, and bring it to a close. This book focuses on helping Korean language learners understand and become accustomed to Korean speech habits and conversational flow.

In **100 Korean Speech Patterns** common speech habits frequently used in everyday Korean conversations are presented through lines from Korean dramas and organized into two sections: Expressions and Sentence Patterns. Although dramas are fictional, the ways in which characters speak and interact closely reflect real-life language use. Following expressions within the context of a scene allows learners to naturally develop a sense of the language—something that is difficult to achieve through grammatical explanations alone.

Each unit begins by introducing the context in which the expressions and patterns are used through illustrations and dialogue from drama scenes. This is followed by short quizzes that encourage learners to think independently about the meaning and usage of the expressions. Detailed explanations of each expression or pattern are then provided, along with example dialogues that demonstrate how they are used in actual conversation. In addition, learners can access audio recordings via QR codes to practice not only meaning but also intonation and nuance in a more vivid and realistic way.

Ms. Sunhee Ryu also contributed to the writing of this book, sharing her keen sense of real-world language use through close interaction with students learning Korean at Ruhr-University Bochum in Germany. I would also like to express my sincere gratitude to the editorial team of Darakwon's Korean Book Publishing Department, who carefully refined each sentence and offered thoughtful guidance throughout the book's structure and editing process. With their efforts, it would have been possible to weave together such lively, screen-like language as presented here.

Rather than aiming for rapid acquisition of speaking skills, this book seeks to help learners become comfortable with the situations in which Korean is spoken. For this reason, we encourage you not to read the material just once, but to revisit it repeatedly—listening, speaking, and practicing until the expressions come to mind naturally. When you later hear these expressions while watching Korean dramas, or find yourself using them effortlessly in conversation, you will gain confidence in your learning.

일러두기

100 Korean Speech Patterns는 크게 2개의 파트로 구성된 책으로 Part 1은 '말 습관 표현', Part 2는 '말 습관 문형'으로 구분하여 K-Drama 속에서 사용된 표현과 문형 100가지를 소개하고 있다. 표현 및 문형이 사용된 대사와 장면을 예시로 보여 주고, 다양한 맥락의 예시 대화문으로 풍부한 학습이 가능하다.

QR 코드

학습할 표현 및 문형, 예문과 대화문을 전문 성우의 생생한 음성으로 QR 코드를 통해 확인할 수 있습니다.

도입

K-Drama의 한 장면을 보여 주는 삽화와 인물의 대사를 통해 먼저 단원에서 학습할 표현 및 문형이 어떤 맥락에서 사용되는지 유추해 봅니다.

Quiz!?

본격적인 학습을 시작하기 전에 간단한 Quiz를 통해 표현 및 문형의 의미와 쓰임새를 추측해 봅니다.

Meaning & Use

표현 및 문법이 어떤 상황과 맥락에서 활용되는지 자세한 설명을 담고 있습니다. 특히 Part 2 에서는 문형을 구조적으로 분석하고 있어 문법 활용의 이해를 도왔습니다.

-길래

-길래 is a casual expression used to explain reasons based on 'personal evidence' that stem from directly seeing, hearing, or feeling a situation or sensation. Grammatically, it is the casual form of -기에, but its stronger subjective and experiential nuance makes it frequently used in natural everyday conversations. Compared to -아/어서 which conveys relatively objective reasons, -길래 gives off the impression that a certain action was taken after observing and judging a situation. It is attached to the stem of a verb or adjective, and to 이다, the stem of a verbal noun, or the endings -으시- and -었- between close acquaintances in everyday conversations.

A 아침에 왜 그렇게 서둘렀어? 무슨 일 있었어?
Why were you in such a hurry in the morning? What happened?

B 버스가 안 *오길래* 택시를 타고 왔어. 그래도 늦었지 뭐.
I took a taxi as the bus wasn't coming. Still ended up late, though.

A 다음엔 좀 더 여유 있게 나오는 게 좋겠네.
Next time, you should leave with a bit more time to spare.

A 무슨 *일이길래* 이렇게 시끄러운 거예요?
What's the commotion (as it sounds chaotic)?

B 이웃에서 불이 날 뻔했나 봐요. 소방차가 왔지만 큰불이 아니라 금방 꺼졌대요.
Looks like there almost was a fire at our neighbor's place. Fire trucks came, but it wasn't a big blaze and they put it out quickly.

A 너 왜 갑자기 집에 간 거야? 연락도 없이.
Why did you suddenly go home? Without even contacting me.

B 비가 엄청 *오길래* 그냥 일찍 들어갔어. 밖에 더 있으면 완전 다 젖을 것 같더라고.
I just went home as it started pouring. I figured if I stayed out longer, I'd get completely soaked.

121

Action!

예시 대화문을 통해 표현 및 문형이 사용되는 다양한 맥락을 이해할 수 있습니다. 음원을 듣고 마치 배우처럼 실제 연기를 하듯 따라 읽으면서 연습해 보세요!

Quiz의 정답과 도입 대사 영어 번역, Meaning & Use 한국어 번역, K-Drama 색인과 100개의 표현 및 문형의 가나다 순 색인이 수록되어 있습니다.

How to Use This Book

"100 Korean Speech Patterns" is a book divided into two main parts: Part 1 covers "Speech Expressions" and Part 2 covers "Speech Patterns". It introduces 100 expressions and patterns used in K-Drama. It provides examples of the dialogue and scenes where the expressions and patterns are used, enabling rich learning through sample dialogues in various contexts.

QR code

Expressions and patterns to learn, example sentences, and dialogues can be accessed via QR code with vivid audio recordings by professional voice actors.

Warm up

Through illustrations depicting a scene from a K-Drama and the characters' dialogue, infer the context in which the expressions and patterns in each unit are used.

Quiz!?

Before beginning the main lesson, take a brief quiz to guess the meaning and usage of expressions and patterns.

Meaning & Use

It provides detailed explanations of how expressions and patterns are used in specific situations and contexts. Part 2, in particular, offers structural analysis of sentence patterns, enabling practical Korean language learning.

-길래 is a casual expression used to explain reasons based on 'personal evidence' that stem from directly seeing, hearing, or feeling a situation or sensation. Grammatically, it is the casual form of -기에, but its stronger subjective and experiential nuance makes it frequently used in natural everyday conversations. Compared to -아/어서 which conveys relatively objective reasons, -길래 gives off the impression that a certain action was taken after observing and judging a situation. It is attached to the stem of a verb or adjective, and to 이다, the stem of a verbal noun, or the endings -으시- and -었- between close acquaintances in everyday conversations.

A 아침에 왜 그렇게 서둘렀어? 무슨 일 있었어?
Why were you in such a hurry in the morning? What happened?

B 버스가 안 **오길래** 택시를 타고 왔어. 그래도 늦었지 뭐.
I took a taxi as the bus wasn't coming. Still ended up late, though.

A 다음엔 좀 더 여유 있게 나오는 게 좋겠네.
Next time, you should leave with a bit more time to spare.

A 무슨 **일이길래** 이렇게 시끄러운 거예요?
What's the commotion (as it sounds chaotic)?

B 이웃에서 불이 날 뻔했나 봐요. 소방차가 왔지만 큰불이 아니라 금방 꺼졌대요.
Looks like there almost was a fire at our neighbor's place. Fire trucks came, but it wasn't a big blaze and they put it out quickly.

A 너 왜 갑자기 집에 간 거야? 연락도 없이.
Why did you suddenly go home? Without even contacting me.

B 비가 엄청 **오길래** 그냥 일찍 들어갔어. 밖에 더 있으면 완전 다 젖을 것 같더라고.
I just went home as it started pouring. I figured if I stayed out longer, I'd get completely soaked.

121

Action!

Through example dialogues, learners can understand the various contexts in which expressions and patterns are used. Listen to the audio and practice by reading along as if you were an actor performing the lines!

This book contains the answers for the quizzes and introductory lines in English translation, meaning and usage in Korean translation, K-Drama index, and an alphabetical index of 100 expressions and patterns.

차례 Table of Contents

Part 1 말 습관 표현 Speech Expressions

Part 2 말 습관 문형
Speech Patterns

부록
Appendix

Meaning & Use
Quiz !?
Action!

Action!
Part 1
말 습관 표현
Speech Expressions
Meaning & Use
Quiz !?

MP3 001

있잖아

You know...

〈폭싹 속았수다〉 (2025)

다음 중 '있잖아'를 사용할 수 있는 가장 적절한 상황은?

In which of the following situations is "있잖아" best used?

ⓐ 회의에서 매니저가 자세한 지시를 내리려고 할 때
ⓑ 학생이 수업 시간에 큰소리로 책을 읽기 시작할 때
ⓒ 누군가 비밀을 말하기 전에 상대의 주의를 끌려고 할 때

Meaning & Use~

있잖아 is combined of 있다 and 잖아. It's used when trying to get the attention of someone else or when beginning a conversation based on a topic the listener already knows. Similar expressions that are used to catch the attention of someone else before raising an important topic include 아니, 그게··· (It's not that...), 저기··· (Hey there...), etc. When -잖아 is used at the end of a sentence, as in "네가 했잖아." (You did it, didn't you?), "춥잖아." (It's cold, isn't it?), it gives off the impression of confirming by means of a question or emphasizing a fact already known. When 있잖아 is used on its own at the beginning of a sentence, it grabs the listener's attention in a strong way, as in "내 말 좀 들어 봐." (Listen to what I have to say.). It's especially often used in romantic confessions: 있잖아 catches the attention of someone else before revealing one's feelings and is followed by a confession like "너를 좋아해." (I like you) or "사랑해." (Love you).

Action!

A *(긴장한 모습으로)* **있잖아**, 나 너한테 할 말이 있어.
(In a nervous state) You know, I have something to tell you.

B 뭔데? What is it?

A 나 너를 좋아해. I like you.

A **있잖아**, 너랑 같이 있으면 너무 편해.
You know, I feel so comfortable when I'm with you.

B 고마워, 나도 그래.
Thank you, me too.

A 너를 사랑하게 된 것 같아.
I think I've come to love you.

A **있잖아**, 너 요즘 많이 힘들어 보여. 무슨 일 있어?
You know, it seems like your having a hard time these days. you seem to be having a hard time lately. Did something happen?

B 응···. 사실 걱정되는 일이 있어. 엄마가 많이 아프셔.
Yeah... In fact, I'm worried about something. My mom is really sick.

02

MP3 002

저기요

Hey there... / Excuse me...

〈사내맞선〉 (2022)

다음 중 '저기요'를 사용할 수 있는 가장 적절한 상황은?

In which situation would it be best to use "저기요"?

ⓐ 전화로 회사에 문의할 때

ⓑ 친구에게 물건을 빌려달라고 할 때

ⓒ 길에서 모르는 사람에게 길을 물어볼 때

Meaning & Use

저기요 (Hey there) is a polite expression used to get the attention of someone (such as strangers or service workers) you don't know well. It's often used in public settings when asking for directions, calling for a waiter in a restaurant, or used towards those who are of similar age or younger than you. It's especially useful when you don't know the other person's name or can't think of a proper title to call them by. Notable examples include trying to get the attention of someone, pointing something out, or starting a conversation. Similar expressions include 저 (Um), 실례합니다 (Excuse me), 여기요 (Over here), etc. Phrases like 잠시만요 (Hold on) and 잠깐만요 (Hang on a moment) are also frequently used to get someone's attention while hoping for their understanding. 저기 is less formal than 저기요, and is often used to get the attention of close friends or colleagues or to start a conversation. It is also useful when you can't immediately remember the other person's name or are uncertain what title to call them by.

Action!

A **저기요**, 실례하지만 이 근처에 지하철역이 어디 있나요?
Excuse me, but where is the nearest subway station?

B 저쪽으로 직진하시면 오른쪽에 있어요.
It's straight down there, to the right.

A *(카페에서 핸드폰을 놓고 자리를 뜨는 사람에게)* **저기요**, 핸드폰 두고 가신 것 같아요.
(When approaching someone who left their phone behind at a cafe) Excuse me, I think you left your phone behind.

B 아이고, 내 정신이야. 하마터면 놓고 갈 뻔 했어요. 정말 감사합니다.
Oh my, I'm losing my mind. I almost left it behind. Thanks a lot.

식당에서 In a restaurant

A **여기요**, 메뉴판 좀 볼 수 있을까요? Over here! May I see the menu?

B 네, 잠시만 기다려 주세요. Sure. Please wait a moment.

A **저기**, 너한테 물어볼 게 있어.
Hey there, I have a question.

B 뭔데? What is it?

MP3 003

미안하지만 / 죄송하지만

Sorry, but...

〈다 이루어질지니〉 (2025)

'미안하지만' 또는 '죄송하지만'을 사용할 수 있는 적절한 상황은?

In which situation would it be best to use "미안하지만" or "죄송하지만"?

ⓐ 친구에게 단순히 인사할 때

ⓑ 친구에게 중요한 부탁을 할 때

ⓒ 직장에서 부하 직원을 꾸짖을 때

미안하지만 and 죄송하지만 are expressions that combine 미안, which expresses discomfort and shame toward the other person, and 죄송, which expresses a more polite feeling of guilt, with the conjunctive adverb 하지만. 하지만 functions to connect contradictory facts. This expression is often used to soften the tone and be considerate of someone else's feelings when requesting help, refusing help, or initiating a conversation that is a sensitive topic. 미안하지만 is used in informal speech, while 죄송하지만 is used in formal speech. Similar expressions include 미안한데, 미안합니다만, 죄송합니다만, 실례지만, etc.

Action!

A **미안하지만**, 내일 통계학 교재 좀 빌려줄 수 있어?

Sorry, but could you lend me your statistics textbook tomorrow?

B 물론이지, 나는 그 과목 시험 다 끝났으니까 천천히 보고 돌려줘.

Sure thing. I'm done with that course's exams, so feel free to take your time and return it whenever is best.

A **죄송하지만**, 오늘은 약속을 지키기 어려울 것 같아요.

I'm sorry, but I don't think I'll be able to follow through with our appointment today.

B 괜찮아요, 그럼 시간이 될 때 다시 약속 잡아요.

No worries. We can reschedule it when you have time.

은행에서 At the bank

A **죄송하지만**, 이 서류를 다시 확인해 주실 수 있나요?

Sorry, but would you be able to double-check this document for me?

B 네, 바로 확인해 드리겠습니다.

Yes, I'll take a look at it right away.

04

가만히 있어 봐

Hold on / Wait

〈무빙〉 (2023)

다음 중 '가만히 있어 봐'를 사용할 수 있는 가장 적절한 상황은?

In which situation would it be best to use "가만히 있어 봐"?

ⓐ 문제를 해결하기 위해 잠깐 집중해야 할 때

ⓑ 친구가 무언가를 잘못했을 때 주의를 주려고 할 때

ⓒ 도서관에서 떠드는 학생들에게 조용히 하라고 할 때

Meaning & Use~

가만히 means "to be quiet without moving or saying anything". When combined with 있다, it indicates "remaining as is without taking any action". If -아/어 봐 is added, the expression 가만히 있어 봐 is formed, requesting someone to wait a moment or stay quiet. This phrase is primarily used when sorting out a situation or focusing on something between people who are close, such as friends or family. It's also used when needing time to think deeply. The expression can also be used with a slightly annoyed tone when someone else's words or actions disrupt you. For example, you might say, "정신 사나우니까 가만히 좀 있어 봐." (I'm in a distracted state, so just stay still for a moment.). Similar expressions include "잠깐만," "기다려 봐," "잠시만," etc.

Action!

A *(여행 가방을 싸며)* 가져 갈 것을 가방에 다 던져 넣어 봐.

(When packing travel luggage) Just throw everything you're taking into the bag.

B ***가만히 있어 봐***, 아무거나 가방에 마구 집어 넣지 말고 꼭 필요한 물건인지 생각해 가면서 넣자고.

Hold on, don't just shove anything into the bag. Think about whether it's really necessary before you pack it.

A *(퍼즐을 하며)* 생각보다 어려운데?

(When solving a puzzle) This is harder than I thought?

B ***가만히 있어 봐***, 내가 한번 맞춰 볼게.

Hold on, let me try to solve it.

A *(체스를 두며)* 빨리해. 벌써 몇 분째야?

(When playing chess) Hurry up. How many minutes has it been already?

B ***가만히 있어 봐***, 지금 생각 중이잖아.

Hold on. Can't you see that I'm thinking right now.

A *(한숨 쉬며)* 이러다 밤새겠네.

(Sighing) At this rate, we'll be up all night.

MP3 005

개인적으로

Personally...

〈손해보기 싫어서〉 (2024)

'개인적으로'는 주로 어떤 상황에서 사용되나요?

In which situation is "개인적으로" commonly used?

ⓐ 최종 결정을 내릴 때

ⓑ 자신의 의견을 표현할 때

ⓒ 다른 사람의 의견을 물을 때

개인적으로 is an adverb meaning "in a way directly related to oneself," or "from one's own standpoint." This expression is frequently used when the speaker expresses their own thoughts or perspective on a topic, or offers advice to someone else. The content that follows is premised on being the speaker's subjective judgment rather than a general or objective opinion. It conveys the nuance of this is just my personal view. Similar expressions include "내 생각에는," "내 입장은," etc.

Action!

A 그 영화 어땠어요?
How was that movie?

B 줄거리가 너무 뻔해서 **개인적으로** 재미없었어요.
The plot was way too predictable. I personally didn't find it to be interesting.

A *(잡지 속 모델의 여러 가지 헤어스타일을 보며)* 이 중 어떤 스타일이 좋아?
(When looking at various hairstyles in a magazine) Which style do you like the best?

B 다 좋은데 **개인적으로** 두 번째 모델 같은 깔끔한 스타일이 좋아.
They're all nice, but I personally like the neat look of the second model.

A 요즘 경기가 안 좋아서 주식 투자를 어떻게 해야 할지 모르겠어.
Lately the economy's been in a rut, so I don't know how to invest in stocks.

B 잘 모르지만 **개인적으로** 안전한 게 제일 좋은 것 같아.
I'm not sure either, but personally I think playing it safe is best.

06

MP3 006

솔직히

Honestly... / To be honest...

〈킹더랜드〉 (2023)

다음 중 '솔직히'를 사용할 수 있는 적절한 상황은?

In which situation would it be best to use "솔직히"?

ⓐ 무례하게 말할 때

ⓑ 평범한 안부를 물을 때

ⓒ 상대방에게 비밀을 털어놓을 때

솔직히 implies truthfulness without concealment or falsehood. It's the shortened form of 솔직히 말하면 (honestly speaking) and is often used in colloquial speech when the speaker wants to express their thoughts or facts openly. In particular, it is commonly used when sharing an opinion and/or confessing, criticizing, or complimenting someone in private or sensitive situations. It is also an effective tactic used to shift the conversation's tone and/or introduce an important topic. Similar expressions include 사실은, 진짜로, as well as slang terms such as 찐으로 (often used online and on social media), and 솔까말 (shortened form of 솔직히 까놓고 말해서), among others.

Action!

A ***솔직히***, 이번 영화 별로였어.
To be honest, this movie wasn't that great.

B 나도 그렇게 생각해. I think so too.

A 시험은 잘 봤어? Did you do well on the test?

B 아니, 너무 어려웠어. 그런데 ***솔직히*** 말하면, 내가 공부를 너무 안 해서 어렵게 느껴졌던 것 같아.
No, it was really difficult. But honestly speaking, I think I found it to be difficult because I didn't study enough.

A 괜찮아, 다음에 더 잘하면 돼.
It's okay. You can do better next time.

A 룸메이트랑 잘 지내고 있어?
Are you getting along with your roommates?

B 안 싸우고 잘 지내. 근데 ***솔직히*** 혼자 살고 싶어. 남한테 맞추는 것이 점점 힘들어져.
We don't have any arguments and we get along well. But honestly, I want to live alone. It's getting increasingly tiresome for me to make compromises with others.

MP3 007

아니

No / Uh

〈웰컴투 삼달리〉 (2023-2024)

'아니'를 사용하는 상황이 아닌 것은?

In which situation would you not use "아니"?

ⓐ 질문할 때

ⓑ 머뭇거릴 때

ⓒ 부정적인 대답을 할 때

The original meaning of 아니 is 그렇지 않다 and is used to deny a statement or question someone else makes. However, when speaking, it is also frequently used to express surprise or admiration at an unexpected situation. For example, when asked "벌써 자니?" (Are you asleep already?), you can reply by saying "아니, 아직 안 자." (Uh, not yet.) and you can express shock by saying "아니, 세상에 이런 일이!". In casual talk, it is used to buy time before speaking or grab someone else's attention. In this case, it is often combined with 근데 (but) to form sentences like "아니, 근데 말이야…" which places emphasis on the second half of a sentence. Furthermore, it can also be used to modify or emphasize the first half of a sentence or the portion between nouns, as in "저 집 월세가 30만 원, 아니 10만 원이라 해도 살고 싶지 않다." (I wouldn't want to live in that house even if the monthly rent was 100,000 won, let alone 300,000 won.)

Action!

A *(초콜릿 칩을 주며)* 이거 하나 먹어 볼래? 맛있어 보여서 샀어.

(When giving chocolate chips) Want one? I bought this because it looked delicious.

B ***아니***, 괜찮아. 다이어트 중이야.

No, I'm good. I'm on a diet.

A *(PC 방에서 나오는 아들을 보고)* ***아니*** 근데 네가 왜 거기서 나와? 학원 간다고 하지 않았어?

(When seeing her son coming out of an internet cafe) Uh, but why are you coming out of there? Didn't you say you were going to the academy?

B 친구 찾으러 왔었어요. 게임한 거 아니에요!

I came to find a friend. I wasn't playing games!

A 주말에 뭐 했어? What did you over the weekend?

B 집에 있었지 뭐…. ***아니***, 근데 말이야, 지난번에 얘기했던 영화 있잖아? 나 그거 드디어 봤어!

I was at home, you know.... Uh, but by the way, remember that movie we talked about last time? I finally saw it!

MP3 008

그러니까

So... / In other words...

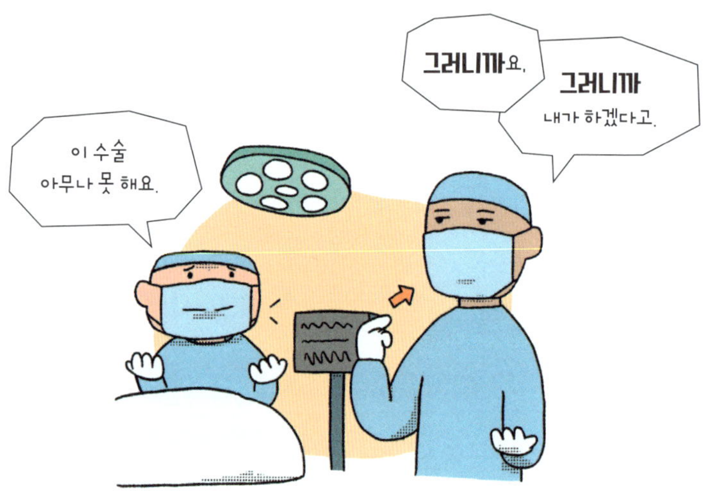

〈중증외상센터〉 (2025)

'그러니까'가 사용될 수 있는 상황을 모두 고르세요.

Choose all the situations in which "그러니까" can be used.

ⓐ 이유나 설명을 덧붙일 때

ⓑ 이해한 내용을 확인할 때

ⓒ 상대방의 말에 동의할 때

그러니까 means 그런 이유로 (based on that reason) or 다시 말해서 (that is to say) and is used to highlight that the first half of the sentence serves as a basis for the second half of the sentence. It's often used to clarify an explanation, summarize something in brief, or emphasize an important point.
It is also used to get the ball rolling in a conversation. For instance, "그러니까 네 말은…" (So what you're saying is...) is used to confirm whether you understood the other person correctly. Additionally, it can be used to agree or relate with what the other person said,, as in "이 바지 너무 크지 않아?" (Aren't these pants too big?) – "그러니까." (Exactly). In this case, it carries a meaning that is similar to "맞아." (Right), "그러게 말이다." (You're telling me).

Action!

A **그러니까** 이런 상황에서는 침착해야 돼요.
So, in situations like this, you have to stay calm.

B 알겠어요, 너무 당황해서 그랬어요.
I know. I was just really flustered.

A **그러니까** 네 말은 우리가 내일까지 이 프로젝트를 끝내야 한다는 거지?
So, you're saying that we have to finish this project by tomorrow, right?

B 맞아. 그렇지 않으면 마감일을 놓치게 돼.
Right. Otherwise we'll miss the deadline.

A 물가가 너무 올라서 알바로만 벌어서는 살아가기 너무 힘드네.
The price of things have gone up so much that it's really tough to get by just on a part-time job.

B *(한숨 쉬며)* **그러니까**…. (Sighing) Exactly....

MP3 009

그런 것 같아

It seems like that... / I guess so...

〈선재 업고 튀어〉 (2024)

다음 중 '그런 것 같아'를 사용할 수 있는 가장 적절한 상황은?

In which situation would it be best to use "그런 것 같아"?

ⓐ 명령을 내릴 때

ⓑ 누군가의 의견에 동의할 때

ⓒ 상대방을 설득하려고 할 때

그런 것 같아 is an expression that is used when conveying something to be somewhat likely based on information they have personally observed or heard. It is frequently used to share an opinion or gently agree with someone else without making a definitive statement. Depending on the situation, it can function as a cautious speculation or serve as a tactic to keep the conversation flowing smoothly. It is particularly effective for minimizing conflicts in opinion or gently responding to what someone else has said. Similar expressions include phrases of aknowledgement, "그럴 수도 있어.", or validation, "맞는 것 같아.".

Action!

A 이 식당 진짜 인기 많아 보이지 않아?
Doesn't this restaurant look really popular?

B 응, **그런 것 같아**. 줄이 엄청 길어.
Yeah, I guess so. The line is crazy long.

A 저 분, 우리 학교 선생님 아니세요?
Isn't that person our school teacher?

B **그런 것 같아요**. 어디서 뵌 분 같네요.
I guess so. I feel like I've met that person before.

A 오늘 발표, 조금 부족했던 것 같지 않아?
Don't you think that my presentation was a bit lacking?

B 응, **그런 것 같아**. 그래도 전달하려던 건 모두 **말한 것 같아**.
Yeah, I guess so. But, I think we said everything we wanted to get across.

MP3 010

10

그치?

Right? / Isn't it?

〈경이로운 소문 2〉 (2023)

'그치?'를 사용할 수 있는 상황은?

In which situation would you use "그치?"?

ⓐ 화를 낼 때

ⓑ 감사를 표현할 때

ⓒ 상대방의 확인을 구할 때

Meaning & Use~

그치 is the shortened form of 그렇지 and is used when acknowledging or agreeing that something is true. It's used to seek agreement from the listener or to confirm whether one's own statement is correct. It's frequently used to emphasize or confirm shared experiences or opinions in a casual way among close colleagues or friends. It can also be used similarly as "그렇지 않아?", the shorted form being "그치 않아?" to convey various nuances such as confirming empathy in a subtle manner, checking the truth of a statement, or verifying in a playful tone. Similar expressions include the colloquial "그츄?", "그렇지 않아요?", and "맞죠?" (Right?). It's also used similarly as the following abbreviated slang: ㅇㅈ? (= 인정? (Agree?)), ㄹㅇ? (= 레알? (Real?)), etc. It can also function as a rhetorical question, similarly to phrases like "아닌가?" (Isn't it?), which gently confirms something.

A 이 노래 진짜 좋다. ***그치?***
This song is so good. Right?

B 응, 요즘 내가 제일 자주 듣는 노래야.
Yeah, it's the one I listen to the most lately.

A 여기 분위기 정말 좋다.
The vibe here is really nice.

B ***그치?*** 사진 찍기 딱 좋은 장소야.
Right? It's the perfect spot to take pictures.

A 떡볶이와 어묵의 조화! 역시 환상이다, ***그치 않아?***
The combination of tteokbokki and fish cakes! It's fantastic, right?

B 맞아, 이 집은 분식집 중 최고인 것 같아.
You're right. I think this place is the best snack bar.

MP3 011

정말?

Really?

〈멜로무비〉 (2025)

'정말?'을 사용할 수 있는 가장 적절한 상황은?

In which situation would it be best to use "정말?"?

ⓐ 칭찬을 할 때

ⓑ 명령을 내릴 때

ⓒ 의심을 표현할 때

정말? is an interrogative expression used to ask whether something is true or not, conveying surprise, disbelief, or a request for confirmation. Depending on the situation, it can be spoken in an excited, skeptical, or neutral tone. Although it takes the form of a question, it simply serves as a rhetorical question that does not seek an answer. A similar expression is the more colloquial and friendly 진짜?. 정말 can also function as a marker of emphasis in a non-question sentence. For example, it is used to intensify the emotional reaction or reinforce the degree of something, as in "내년에는 정말 국내 여행이라도 한 번 갔으면 좋겠어." (I really hope I can take at least one trip domestically next year) or "신부가 정말 눈부시게 아름답다." (The bride is really dazzlingly beautiful.). A similar expression is "정말로?". This expression, however, is more readily used when confirming facts that are hard to believe.

Action!

A 나 드디어 승진했어! I finally got promoted!

B **정말?** 축하해! Really? Congratulations!

A 내일은 **정말** 바다를 보고 싶어.
I really want to see the sea tomorrow.

B 그럼 내일 아침 일찍 출발하자.
Then let's leave early tomorrow morning.

A 와, 신부가 **정말로** 눈부시게 아름답다.
Wow, the bride is really dazzlingly beautiful.

B 그러게, 눈을 뗄 수가 없네.
Tell me about it. I can't take my eyes off her.

A 나 어제 로또 1등 당첨됐어.
I won the lottery yesterday.

B **정말로?** 에이… 농담이지?
Really? No way... You're kidding around, right?

12

MP3 012

아깝다

What a shame/waste

〈슬기로운 의사생활 1〉 (2020)

다음 중 '아깝다'를 사용할 수 있는 상황은?

In which situation can you use "아깝다"?

ⓐ 기뻐할 때

ⓑ 귀중한 것을 잃었을 때

ⓒ 복잡한 문제를 설명할 때

Meaning & Use~

아깝다 is an expression meaning "feeling disappointed and regretful when things don't go as planned, or feeling regretful about losing something valuable or wasting it." It expresses the regret and disappointment felt when losing something precious or missing an opportunity, and is primarily used when time, money, effort, or opportunities are wasted in vain. It is also frequently used when losing a game by a narrow margin or failing at the last moment after nearly accomplishing or winning something. Similar, yet distinct expressions include 안타깝다 (regrettable) and 아쉽다 (disappointing). 안타깝다 expresses anguish when things don't go as planned or when something is pitiful, and 안타깝게도 means 불행히도 (unfortunately). On the other hand, 아쉽다 expresses dissatisfaction when something needed is missing or insufficient, or a lingering sense of regret. It can also be used in light-heartedly. For example, "비빔밥에 계란이 빠져서 아쉽네." (It's a bummer that an egg was left out of the bibimbap.).

Action!

A 새로 산 핸드폰을 잃어버렸어.
I lost my new phone.

B ***아깝다***. 한 달 밖에 못 썼잖아.
What a waste. You only used it for a month.

A 지호가 또 운전면허 시험에서 떨어졌대. 근데 이번엔 진짜 아까워. 한 문제 차이로 떨어진 거래.
Jiho failed his driver's test again. But this time it's really unfortunate. He failed by just one question.

B 또? ***안타깝네***…. 지호도 정말 실망이 크겠다. 다음에는 붙을 거야, 힘내라고 전해 줘.
Again? What a shame.... Jiho must be really disappointed. Tell him he'll pass next time, and to keep trying.

A 오늘 회의에 김 차장님 못 오신다네.
General Manager Kim can't make it to today's meeting.

B ***아쉽다***. 좋은 의견을 많이 들을 수 있었을 텐데.
What a shame. We could have gotten a lot of good opinions from him.

13

MP3 013

뭐랄까

How should I put it...

〈어쩌다 발견한 하루〉 (2019)

'뭐랄까'를 사용할 수 있는 상황은?

In which situation can "뭐랄까" be used?

ⓐ 말을 시작할 때

ⓑ 누군가를 칭찬할 때

ⓒ 정확히 표현하기 어려운 느낌을 전달할 때

뭐랄까 is the shortened form of 뭐라고 할까 and is used when it's difficult to express something in words or find the right phrasing. It's used to buy time to gather one's thoughts or to convey thoughts or feelings that are hard to explain easily. Variations include "뭐라고 해야 할까," "뭐라고 하면 좋을까," "뭐라 하지...."

Action!

A 이 작품을 보고 있으면 **뭐랄까**, 왠지 울고 싶은 기분이 든다고 해야 하나? 그런 묘한 감정이 들어.

When I look at this piece... How would I put it? Would I say it somehow makes me feel like crying? It stirs up strange emotions.

B 무슨 말인지 알 것 같아. 나도 기분이 좀 이상해지더라고.

I think I know what you mean. I feel a bit strange too.

A 새로운 직장에 다니게 된 기분이 어떠세요?

How do you feel about starting at your new job?

B **뭐랄까**··· *(어떻게 표현해야 할지 잠시 고민하며)* 기쁘기도 하고 걱정되기도 해요.

How would I put it... (pausing to consider how to express it) I'm happy, but also concerned.

A 어제 소개팅에서 만난 사람 어때?

How was the person you met on the blind date yesterday?

B **뭐랄까**··· *(적절한 단어를 고르며)* 차분하면서도 카리스마 있는 사람 같아.

How would I put it... (searching for the right words) He comes across as a calm yet charismatic person, I guess.

14

MP3 014

대박!

Awesome! / Wow!

〈엄마친구아들〉 (2024)

'대박!'을 사용할 수 있는 가장 적절한 상황은?

Which of the following is an appropriate situation to use "대박!"?

ⓐ 슬플 때

ⓑ 상대방을 혼낼 때

ⓒ 좋은 소식을 들었을 때

Meaning & Use~

대박! is a colloquial expression used to express surprise, admiration, or excitement at an unexpected event or astonishing outcome. It figuratively signifies that something significant has been achieved. Primarily used in informal situations, its meaning can vary depending on the speaker's tone or expression, and can be used both positive and negative contexts. It can also be modified into forms like 대박이다 (It's a big hit) or 대박 사건 (A big hit event). Similar expressions include 와, 대단하다! (Wow, that is amazing!) or 우와! (Wow). When expressing surprise in its simplest form, slang like "헐" (whoa) or "진짜?" (really?) are frequently used.

Action!

A 이 가방이 80% 세일 중이래!
They said this bag is 80% off!

B *대박!* 나도 하나 사야겠다.
Wow! I should get one too.

A 삼촌, 저 이번에 그림 대회에서 1등 했어요!
Uncle, I won first place in the drawing contest this time!

B *대박!* 너 그림 진짜 잘 그리는구나!
Wow! You really draw well!

A *대박!* 방금 하늘에서 UFO를 봤어.
Wow! I just saw a UFO in the sky.

B 헐, 진짜야? 제대로 본 것 맞아?
Whoa, really? Are you sure you actually saw one?

MP3 015

15

짜증나

I'm annoyed

〈갯마을 차차차〉 (2021)

'짜증나'를 사용할 수 있는 가장 적절한 상황은?

In which situation would it be best to use "짜증나"?

ⓐ 감사할 때

ⓑ 친구와 논의할 때

ⓒ 화가 나거나 귀찮을 때

짜증나다 means "to feel annoyed or frustrated because something does not live up to your expectations or is irritating." In casual contexts, it is often shortened to 짜증나, which express dissatisfaction, anger, or frustration. It is frequently used when things don't go as planned, when one is disrupted, or when displeased with someone's words, actions, or a situation. To emphasize feeling annoyed, one might say "짜증난다고!" (I said that I'm annoyed!). When directly expressing dissatisfaction to someone else, the expression "정말 짜증나게 왜 이래?" (Are you going to annoy me like this?). It's also frequently muttered as a complaint when things don't go as desired, primarily among friends or close acquaintances. Similar expressions include "화나." (I'm angry) and "열받아." (I'm furious).

A 도로가 완전 막혔어.
The road is jammed.

B 아, **짜증나**! 결혼식에 늦겠어.
Ugh, I'm annoyed! I'm gonna be late for the wedding.

A 인터넷이 또 끊겼어.
The internet's down again.

B 진짜? **짜증나네**. 인터넷 서비스 업체를 바꿔 볼까?
Really? It's annoying. Should we switch internet providers?

A 헐, 오늘 수연이랑 영화 보기로 했는데 깜빡했네.
Whoa, I completely forgot I was supposed to see a movie with Sooyeon today.

B 뭐? 너 지난번에도 그러지 않았어? 수연이 엄청 **짜증났겠다**. 빨리 가 봐.
What? Didn't you do that last time too? Sooyeon must be really annoyed. You better hurry over.

16

MP3 016

헐

Whoa / Oh my god

〈오징어 게임 2〉 (2025)

'헐'을 사용할 수 있는 적절한 상황은?

In which situation would it be best to use "헐"?

ⓐ 충격을 받았을 때

ⓑ 상대방을 칭찬할 때

ⓒ 새로운 친구를 소개할 때

헐 is an interjection used in casual conversation when something is so absurd or ridiculous it leaves you speechless, when encountering a surprising or shocking situation, or when witnessing or hearing an unbelievable fact or scene. It can be used in both positive and negative contexts, and is sometimes combined with 대박 in the form of "헐, 대박." to express a stronger emotional reaction. Similar expressions include "와" (Wow), "진짜?" (really), etc.

Action!

A 이 옷이 300만 원이래.
They said this dress costs 3,000,000 won.

B 헐, 진짜 비싸다! Whoa, that's really expensive!

A 수진이 다음 달에 결혼한대.
Sujin is getting married next month.

B 헐, 남자 친구 생긴 지 얼마 안 되지 않았어?
Whoa, didn't she just start dating her boyfriend?

A 성진이가 오늘 큰 사고를 당했대.
Sungjin was in a major accident today.

B 헐, 진짜? 무슨 사고? 성진이는 괜찮대?
Whoa, really? What kind of accident? Is Sungjin alright?

A 나 이번에 수영 대회에서 1등했어!
I won first place in the swimming competition this time!

B 헐, 대박. 정말 축하해! 작년부터 열심히 준비하더니 결국 1등을 했구나!
Wow, that's amazing! Congratulations! You've been working hard since last year, and you finally came in first!

MP3 017

말도 안 돼

No way, Unbelievable

〈스물다섯 스물하나〉 (2022)

'말도 안 돼'의 뜻과 가장 비슷한 표현은?

Which expression is most similar to "말도 안 돼"?

ⓐ 진짜요?

ⓑ 고마워요.

ⓒ 실례합니다.

말도 안 된다 means "it doesn't make sense or it's unreasonable." In casual conversations, it's primarily used as 말도 안 돼 to express disbelief or surprise at someone's words or a situation. It's frequently used as a reaction of shock or doubt in unexpected situations, whether positive or negative. It comes naturally when achieving an unexpectedly good result, securing a dramatic victory in a game, or encountering an incomprehensible situation or hearing absurd news. Similar expressions include "진짜?" (Really?), "세상에!" (What in the world!), "거짓말!" (You must be lying!), etc.

Action!

A 동생이 복권에 당첨됐어!
My younger sibling won the lottery!

B **말도 안 돼**! 진짜?
No way! Really?

A 영화 '문어 게임'에 나온 이춘자 배우있지? 은퇴한대.
You know Lee Chun-ja, the actress from the movie "Octopus Game"? She's retiring.

B **말도 안 돼**. 이제 겨우 서른 넘었잖아. 무슨 은퇴?
No way. She's just turned thirty. What do you mean, retiring?

A 우리 강아지가 냉장고 문을 열었어.
My dog opened the refrigerator door.

B 헐, **말도 안 돼**! 나보고 그걸 믿으라고?
Whoa, no way! You expect me to believe that?

MP3 018

18

그렇긴 한데

That's true, but...

〈킹더랜드〉 (2023)

'그렇긴 한데'를 사용할 수 있는 가장 적절한 상황은?

In which situation would it be best to use "그렇긴 한데"?

ⓐ 화를 낼 때

ⓑ 상대방의 의견을 완전히 부정할 때

ⓒ 상대방의 의견에 동의는 하지만 추가 의견이 있을 때

Meaning & Use~

그렇긴 하다 is an expression that is used when "acknowledging someone else's stance or agreeing in part with a particular fact, but adding another perspective or condition." In casual conversations, it is often used as 그렇긴 한데… (That's true, but...) in order to acknowledge someone else's opinion while gently presenting a different viewpoint. It is effective when accepting a fact while adding differing, supplemental thoughts, softening a rebuttal, or sharing feedback in a cautious way. It is also used to appease someone else who expresses dissatisfaction or to lighten an intense situation. Similar expressions include "맞긴 한데" (You are right, but...), "그렇지," "그런데..." (Right, but...), etc.

Action!

A 이 웹툰 진짜 재밌지?

This webtoon is really enjoyable, isn't it?

B ***그렇긴 한데***, 마지막 에피소드는 별로였어. 억지로 짜 맞춘 느낌이랄까?

That's true, but the last episode was kinda meh. It felt forced, as if they were trying too hard to make the story come together.

A 이번 프로젝트 계획은 완벽한 것 같아요.

This project plan seems perfect.

B ***그렇긴 한데요***, 인원이 부족해서 제대로 실행할 수 있을지 모르겠어요.

That's true, but we're short on staff, so I'm not sure if it'll actually work out.

A 저 사람 뷔랑 닮았어.

That person looks like V.

B ***그렇긴 한데***, 뷔라고 하기에는 키가 너무 크다.

That's true, but he's too tall to be V.

19

MP3 019

완전

Total(ly) / Complete(ly)

〈옥씨부인전〉 (2024-2025)

'완전'의 의미와 가장 가까운 단어는?

Which of the following words has a meaning that is closest to "완전"?

ⓐ 전혀

ⓑ 매우

ⓒ 천천히

Meaning & Use~

완전 means "being fully complete without any lack or flaw." In casual conversations, it goes beyond this meaning and is used to add emphasis to something. It can be used in both positive and negative contexts among friends or close acquaintances to convey a sense of admiration or share an opinion in an emphatic way. It frequently appears when expressing personal preferences or feelings. However, in formal situations or official documents, it is more appropriate to use expressions like 정말, 아주, or 매우. Similar informal expressions include 진짜, 엄청, etc.

Action!

A 이거 진짜 맛있지?
This is really delicious, isn't it?

B 응, **완전** 맛있어!
Yeah, it's totally delicious!

A 어제 본 영화 어땠어?
How was the movie you saw yesterday?

B **완전** 대박이었어.
It was totally awesome.

A 넌 이 옷 진짜 잘 어울려.
This outfit really suits you.

B 고마워! 나도 **완전** 맘에 들어.
Thanks! I too totally like it.

20

MP3 020

뭐라고?

What did you say?

〈런 온〉 (2021)

'뭐라고?'를 사용할 수 있는 가장 적절한 상황은?

In which situation would it be best to use "뭐라고?"?

ⓐ 의견에 동의할 때

ⓑ 누군가를 축하할 때

ⓒ 상대방이 해서는 안 될 말을 했을 때

뭐라고? is used when you want to confirm what you heard as you were either unable to hear someone else clearly or heard something that is hard to believe. It's also used to verify something, but its meaning subtly changes depending on the tone and facial expression. When used with a surprised expression, it conveys disbelief at what was said. When spoken in an angry tone, it implies disapproval or disappointment, suggesting someone said something they shouldn't have. Similar expressions include "뭐?" (What?) and "다시 말해 봐." (Say that again). "무슨 말이야?" (What did you say?) is a more subtle, peaceful form of confirming the meaning or intent of a statement while requesting additional explanation.

Action!

A *(전화 통화 중)* 내일 학교 앞 카페에서 만나.
(When on the phone) Meet me at the cafe in front of the school tomorrow.

B **뭐라고?** 어디서 만나자고? 갑자기 소리가 안 들려서 잘 못 들었어.
What did you say? Where should we meet? I couldn't hear you clearly because the sound cut off suddenly.

A 나 임신했어. I'm pregnant.

B **뭐라고?** 진짜야? 정말 축하해!
What did you say? Really? Congratulations!

A 고마워. Thanks.

A 오늘 저녁 동창회에 못 갈 것 같아.
I don't think I can make it to the reunion tonight.

B **뭐라고?** 친구들이 너를 무척 보고 싶어할 텐데…. 왜 못 가는데?
What did you say? Your friends will really miss you.... Why can't you go?

A 할머니께서 편찮으셔. My grandmother is sick.

A 이봐, 학생. 여기서 담배 피우면 안 되지. Hey, kid. You can't smoke here.

B 에이, 별것도 아닌 걸로 왜 그러세요?
Oh, come on, it's no big deal. Why are you making such a fuss?

A **뭐라고?** 별것 아니라니! 아이들 놀이터 앞에서 뻑뻑 담배를 피우고 있잖아!
What did you say? No big deal?! You're smoking right in front of the playground!!!

21

MP3 021

아무튼

At any rate... / Anyway...

〈나의 완벽한 비서〉 (2025)

'아무튼'을 사용할 수 있는 가장 적절한 상황은?

In which situation would it be best to use "아무튼"?

ⓐ 사과를 할 때

ⓑ 대화를 마무리하고 싶을 때

ⓒ 상대방에게 감사를 표현할 때

아무튼 means "regardless of the situation" and is an informal expression used to summarize a conclusion or wrap up a conversation without dwelling on previously mentioned details. It conveys to the listener that the outcome remains the same regardless of any condition and is also frequently used to shift topics in a light way. Similar expressions include 어쨌든 (anyway), 하여튼 (anyhow), and 그건 그렇고 (that being said). Additionally, 그건 그렇고 is used to smoothly shift from the previous topic to a new one. It retains the flow of the conversation while changing the subject, and is also useful for asking about minor details or drawing attention to an important topic. Similar expressions include "그런데," "참," "그런데 말이야."

Action!

A 이번 프로젝트는 생각보다 어려울 것 같아요.
This project seems harder than I thought.

B 맞아요, 시간이 많이 걸릴 것 같죠? **아무튼**, 최선을 다해 봅시다.
Yeah, it's gonna take a lot of time, right? At any rate, let's do our best.

A 컨디션은 좀 어때? 내일 경기 뛸 수 있겠어?
How are you feeling? Are you able to run at tomorrow's game?

B 아직 별로 좋지 않아. **아무튼** 간에 내일 경기에는 무조건 나갈 거야.
Still not great. But, at any rate, I'm definitely playing tomorrow no matter what.

A 그래서 이 약속이 왜 그렇게 중요한 거야?
So why is this promise so important?

B 벌써 설명했잖아. *(정말 귀찮다는 표정으로)* **아무튼**, 나중에 다시 얘기하자.
I already explained. (with a really annoyed look) At any rate, let's talk about it later.

A 오늘 점심 뭐 먹었어?
What did you have for lunch today?

B 김밥 먹었어. **그건 그렇고**, 너 어제 어디 갔었어?
I had kimbap. That's that, but at any rate, where did you go yesterday?

MP3 022

당연하지

Of course

〈봄밤〉 (2019)

다음 중 '당연하지'의 뜻과 가장 가까운 것은?

Which word has the closest meaning to "당연하지"?

ⓐ 몰라.

ⓑ 아니야.

ⓒ 물론이야.

당연하다 means "it's only natural, not at all surprising" and in casual conversations it's used in the form 당연하지! (Of course!) to express agreement or conviction. It emphasizes complete agreement with someone else's words or their suggestion, or to highlight that the content is clear beyond doubt. Depending on the context, it can convey simple factual acknowledgment, encouragement, or a friendly, playful agreement. It is primarily used informally among close acquaintances like friends or family. Its tone can be serious or lighthearted. Similar expressions include "물론이지" and "그럼." Variations like "당근이지" or the abbreviated form 당근 are widely used to create a cheerful and friendly atmosphere.

Action!

A 나 좀 도와줄래?
Could you give me a hand?

B **당연하지**! 뭐부터 할까?
Of course! What first?

A 이번 주말에 같이 여행 가는 거 어때?
How about we go on a trip together this weekend?

B 좋지. 다른 애들도 부를까?
Sounds good. Should we invite others too?

A **당연하지**, 단톡방에 올릴게.
Of course. I'll post it in the group chat.

A 내일 우리 집에서 파티할 건데 올래?
I'm having a party at my place tomorrow. Want to come?

B **당연하지**, 꼭 갈게. 완전 재밌겠다!
Of course, I'll definitely go. It'll be totally fun!

23

MP3 023

글쎄

Hmm... / Well...

〈Mr. 플랑크톤〉 (2024)

'글쎄'를 사용할 수 있는 상황은?

In which situation would you use "글쎄"?

ⓐ 화를 낼 때

ⓑ 짜증이 날 때

ⓒ 확신이 없을 때

글쎄 is a sound made when unable to readily affirm or deny the other person's question. It is used in casual conversations when hesitating to immediately answer a question or when not immediately agreeing with what someone else said. It is frequently used when uncertain or needing a little bit more time to think. Similar expressions include "잘 모르겠는데" (I'm not sure), "음···" (Hmm...), etc. It can also be used to smoothly connect sentences without any significant meaning. An expression like "아니, 글쎄" (Well, I'm unsure) introduces a new topic, captures attention, and sparks curiosity.

Action!

A 이 책 어때? What do you think of this book?

B **글쎄**···. 나도 아직 안 읽어 봐서 잘 모르겠어.
Hmm.... I haven't read it yet, so I don't know.

A 내일 만날 수 있어?
Can we meet tomorrow?

B **글쎄**, 스케줄 좀 봐야 할 것 같아.
Hmm, I'll have to check my schedule.

A **글쎄**, 오늘 지하철에서 연예인을 만났지 뭐야.
Hmm, you know I ran into a celebrity on the subway today.

B *(두 눈을 반짝이며)* 진짜? 누구였어?
(Eyes sparkling) Really? Who was it?

A RM! 모자를 푹 눌러썼는데도 너무 멋있더라.
RM! He was wearing a hat pulled down low, but he still looked so cool.

MP3 024

어쩌라고?

So what?

〈선재 업고 튀어〉 (2024)

'어쩌라고?'는 주로 어떤 상황에서 사용되나요?

In which situation is "어쩌라고?" mainly used?

ⓐ 감사할 때

ⓑ 동의를 표현할 때

ⓒ 상대방의 말을 무시하거나 짜증을 표현할 때

Meaning & Use~

어쩌다 comes from a verb meaning "to happen by chance or occur unexpectedly," and 어쩌라고? literally translates to "What do you want me to do?". In casual conversations, it's primarily used as an informal expression to show irritation, defiance, or indifference toward someone else's words or actions. It's typically used when the other person's words feel unnecessary or unrelated to the situation, or when their advice or intervention is perceived as excessive/unnecessary. Depending on the tone, it can sound like light-hearted banter, but it often comes across as sharp or cold, so it should be used cautiously depending on the context. It can be used in variations like "아, 어쩌라고?" or "그래서 뭐 어쩌라고?", and sometimes conveys an attitude of "I don't care whether you're right or wrong".

Action!

A 너 또 아이스크림 사 먹었지?
You bought and ate ice cream again, didn't you?

B 응, 그래서 **어쩌라고?** *(웃으며)* 너도 한 입 줄까?
Yeah, so what? (laughing) Do you want a bite, too?

A 네가 그 사람과 사귀면 사람들이 뭐라고 할까?
What will people say if you date that person?

B **어쩌라고?** 내가 좋아하면 그게 중요한 거지.
So what? If I like her, that's what matters.

A 네가 잘못했잖아. You're the one who messed up.

B 그래서 뭐 **어쩌라고?** So what about it?

A 너는 숙제도 안 하고 맨날 게임만 하니?
You don't even do your homework and just play games all day?

B *(날카롭게)* 그래서 뭐, **어쩌라고?**
(In a sharp tone) So what about it?

MP3 025

어쩔 수 없지

It is what it is / It can't be helped

〈너의 시간 속으로〉 (2023)

'어쩔 수 없지'와 비슷한 의미의 표현은?

Which expression has a similar meaning to "어쩔 수 없지"?

ⓐ 당연하지.

ⓑ 방법이 없어.

ⓒ 신경 쓰지 마.

Meaning & Use~

어쩔 수 없어 and 어쩔 수 없지 are expressions used to accept an unavoidable situation and indicate that there is no other choice. Both expressions convey the same meaning, but 어쩔 수 없어 is more commonly used when speaking to oneself or when acknowledging a situation on one's own, while 어쩔 수 없지 is more naturally used to agree with someone else's statement or to acknowledge a situation together with someone else. When plans or things don't turn out as expected, these phrases convey giving up or understanding that there's no alternative. Such expressions can also offer comfort to someone who experiences misfortune, implying "it happens, so don't blame yourself too much". Additionally, they express acceptance of situations that they would ideally like to change but that are realistically impossible to alter or have already been decided. The past tense form 어쩔 수 없었어/없었지 (It couldn't be helped) emphasizes that one had no choice and can be used as an excuse or explanation. Similar expressions include "할 수 없어" (nothing can be done) and "방법이 없어" (there is no way around it).

Action!

A 비가 와서 야외 행사를 못 하게 됐어.
It rained, so we couldn't host the outdoor event.

B *어쩔 수 없지*. 그래도 열심히 준비했는데 많이 아쉬웠겠다.
It can't be helped. Still, you must be really disappointed after preparing so hard.

A 내가 원하는 대로 일이 진행되지 않아서 너무 속상해.
I'm so upset that things aren't going the way I want them to.

B *어쩔 수 없지*, 때로는 우리가 원하는 대로 일이 안 될 때도 있잖아.
It is what it is. Sometimes things just don't go our way.

A 왜 항상 힘든 일은 네가 다 도맡아 하는 거야?
Why do you always end up taking on all the tough tasks?

B *어쩔 수 없어*, 나 밖에 할 사람이 없잖아.
It can't be helped. There's no one else to do it but me.

26

MP3 026

그렇구나

I see

〈Mr. 플랑크톤〉 (2024)

'그렇구나'를 사용할 수 있는 상황은?

In which situation would you use "그렇구나"?

ⓐ 이해가 잘 안 될 때

ⓑ 모르는 것을 질문할 때

ⓒ 무언가를 이해하거나 깨달았을 때

Meaning & Use~

그렇구나 is an everyday expression used to show empathy, understanding, or realization in response to what someone else has said. It serves as a natural reaction when hearing new information. It conveys the meaning of "Oh, now I understand." and helps smoothly continue the conversation. However, in casual conversations among friends, it isn't always used to convey understanding or realization in a serious way. It can be used, therefore, sarcastically with a mocking tone, to lightly brush off a comment or to make a joke. Depending on the intonation and facial expression, it can convey warm empathy or, conversely, a sarcastic undertone. Therefore, it should be used carefully depending on the situation. Using the past tense form "그랬구나" (That's how it was) can convey understanding someone else to a strong degree. Similar expressions include "아, 그래?" and "아, 그렇지?", which respond to and acknowledge what someone else has said.

A 어제 비 때문에 길이 막혔어.
The roads were blocked off because of the rain yesterday.

B **그렇구나**. 그래서 늦게 들어왔구나.
I see. That's why you got back home late.

A 나 다이어트 시작했어.
I started dieting.

B *(익살스럽게 웃으며)* **그렇구나**~. 근데 저 케이크는 뭐야?
(Laughing playfully) I see~. Then what about that cake?

A 이번 시험이 진짜 어려웠어.
This exam was really tough.

B **그렇구나**. 다른 사람들도 그랬을 거야.
I see. Everyone else must have felt the same way.

27

MP3 027

뭔가

Something...

〈은중과 상연〉 (2025)

'뭔가'가 사용될 수 있는 상황은?

In which situation would you use "뭔가"?

ⓐ 칭찬할 때

ⓑ 특정한 것을 명확히 알 때

ⓒ 정확히 모르는 무언가를 표현하고 싶을 때

Meaning & Use~

뭔가 is an abbreviation of 무엇인가 (what is it) or 무언가 and is used very frequently in everyday conversations. It is primarily used when referring to an unspecified object, or when wanting to express a certain feeling or state without precisely knowing about it. Similar expressions that covey an inkling or guess include "왠지" (for some reason), meaning "I can't explain why, but I feel that way," and "뭔지 모르겠지만" (I don't know what it is, but).

Action!

A 저기 이상한 소리 들리지 않아?
Can you hear that weird noise coming from over there?

B 응, **뭔가** 떨어지는 소리 같은데.
Yeah, sounds like something falling.

A 오늘 너 표정이 좀 이상해.
Your facial expressions seem a bit off today.

B 나도 모르겠어, **뭔가** 불안해.
I don't know. I feel uneasy or something.

A 이번 발표 좀 이상하지 않았어?
Didn't that presentation feel weird?

B 왠지 **뭔가** 부족했던 것 같아.
Somehow, it felt like something was missing.

28

MP3 028

지금?

Now?

〈다 이루어질지니〉 (2025)

'지금?'이라는 표현을 사용할 수 있는 상황은?

In which situation would you use "지금?"?

ⓐ 미래 계획을 논의할 때

ⓑ 과거의 일에 대해 묻고 싶을 때

ⓒ 현재 일어나는 상황에 반응할 때

Meaning & Use~

지금 is an adverb meaning "at this very moment." When speaking, it is often used in a brief question form, 지금?, to either confirm or react to an action or event happening immediately, to emphasize surprise or urgency at an unexpected timing or situation, or to express awkwardness, embarrassment, or negative feelings. Depending on the intonation and tone, the meaning can range from a friendly counter-question to bewilderment. Similar expressions include "지금 바로?" (Right now?), "당장?" (Immediately?), etc.

Action!

A 나 지금 집 앞이야. I'm in front of your place now.

B *(창밖을 보며)* **지금?** 벌써 왔어?
(Looking out the window) Now? You're already came?

A 발표 순서가 바뀌었어. 지금이 네 차례래.
The presentation order changed. It's your turn now.

B **지금?** 준비도 안 했는데!
Now? I'm not ready!

A 지금 통화 가능해?
Are you available to speak on the phone now?

B **지금?** 곤란해. 도서관이야.
Now? That'll be difficult. I'm at the library.

29

설마

No way / You can't be serious

〈닥터 차정숙〉(2023)

'설마'를 사용할 수 있는 상황은?

In which situation would you use "설마"?

ⓐ 상대방을 칭찬할 때

ⓑ 친구와 인사를 나눌 때

ⓒ 믿기 어려운 소식을 들었을 때

Meaning & Use~

설마 is an expression used when speaking to doubt something or dismiss it outright, often conveying surprise, disbelief, or or bewilderment in colloquial speeches. Depending on the tone and intonation, it can convey a wide range of nuances, from light-hearted banter to serious denial. A similar expression is 그럴 리가 없어 (There's no way). While 설마 gives the impression of a lingering doubt, 그럴 리가 firmly asserts something is logically impossible. For example, "설마, 네가 그걸 잊었어?" (You mean you forgot that?) carries both doubt and surprise, asking "Could that really be true?" whereas "그럴 리가 없어!" (No way!) is an outright denial. Both expressions are used when reacting to an unbelievable situation, but they differ in intensity and tone.

Action!

A 민호가 시험에서 0점을 받았대.
Minho scored a zero on the test.

B 설마! 농담이지?
No way! You're kidding, right?

A 설마, 너 정말 그걸 잊고 있었어?
No way. You really forgot about that?

B 아, 미안. 요즘 너무 바빴어.
Oh, sorry. I've been so busy lately.

A 설마, 네가 정말 그 대회에서 우승했다고?
No way. You really won that competition?

B 맞아, 나도 안 믿겨!
Right, I can't believe it either!

MP3 030

30

혼나다

Almost died...

〈그 여자의 바다〉 (2017)

다음 중 '혼나다'의 의미가 다른 것은 무엇일까요?

Which has a meaning that differs from "혼나다"?

ⓐ 아파서 혼나다

ⓑ 선생님께 혼나다

ⓒ 외로워서 혼나다

혼나다 means "to be scolded to the point of being extremely startled or embarrassed." Combined with -아/어서, the phrase -아/어서 혼나다 is used to emphasize a situation or experience whereby one endures great hardship or suffering. It is synonymous with expressions like 혼꾸멍나다 or 혼쭐이 나다. In everyday contexts, it's used to express significant physical or mental hardship, like "감기에 걸려서 혼났어." (I got a real beating from this cold.), "더워서 혼났어." (I got a real beating from the heat.), or "짜증나서 혼났어." (I got a real beating due to frustration.). Rather than simply saying "힘들었어." (It was hard.), incorporating 혼나다 makes it easier for the listener to empathize with the situation.

Action!

A 주말에 뭐 했어? 얼굴이 완전 피곤해 보이는데.
What did you do over the weekend? You look totally exhausted.

B 장염에 걸려서 일주일 동안 **혼났어**. 설사랑 복통으로 엄청 고생했어.
I got gastroenteritis and was miserable for a week. I almost died from diarrhea and stomach cramps.

A 어제 회의 분위기 어땠어?
How was the atmosphere of the meeting yesterday?

B 서로 말 안 통하고 답답해서 진짜 **혼났어**.
I almost died because we couldn't communicate at all.

A 왜 목소리가 쉬었어? Why's your voice so hoarse?

B 어제 술집에서 친구들 싸움 말리느라 **혼났어**. 목도 다 쉬었네.
I almost died yesterday as I was trying to stop my friends from getting into a fight. My voice is totally gone.

31

MP3 031

약간

A bit... / Slightly...

〈너의 시간 속으로〉 (2023)

'약간'을 사용할 수 있는 상황은?

In which situation would you use "약간"?

ⓐ 정확히 맞을 때

ⓑ 크게 강조하고 싶을 때

ⓒ 조금 애매하거나 약할 때

Meaning & Use~

약간 indicates a small degree or a lack of intensity. It is also frequently used to soften explanations or convey subtle differences. Especially in evaluative situations, it serves to reduce the severity of what might otherwise be a strong impression. The subjective feelings or attitude of the speaker are conveyed implicitly, thereby giving a subtle or gentle impression. Variations include 조금 (a little) and 살짝 (slightly).

Action!

A 오늘 컨디션 어때? How do you feel today?

B 어제 늦게 자서 그런지 **약간** 피곤해.
I'm a bit tired, probably because I stayed up late last night.

A 이 영화 어땠어? How was the movie?

B 내용은 괜찮았는데 **약간** 이상했어. 결말이 좀 뜬금없더라.
The story was okay, but it felt a bit off. The ending was kind of abrupt.

A 이 음식 어때? How's this food?

B 맛있긴 한데 **약간** 짜. 조금만 덜 짰으면 더 좋았을 것 같아.
It's tasty, but a bit salty. It would've been better if it was less salty.

A 이 옷 어때? How does this outfit look?

B 디자인은 괜찮은데, 너한테는 **약간** 큰 것 같아.
The design is nice, but it's a bit big on you.

A 그럼 한 치수 작은 걸 입어 볼까?
Then should I try one size smaller?

32

MP3 032

그거 알지?

Do you catch my drift?

〈미지의 서울〉 (2025)

'그거 알지?'는 어떤 의도로 사용되나요?

With which intent is "그거 알지?" used?

ⓐ 화를 낼 때

ⓑ 혼자 생각할 때

ⓒ 상대방의 동의를 구할 때

알다 is a verb meaning "to recognize or remember an object or fact." In casual conversations, 그거 알지? is primarily used when the speaker assumes the listener already knows something and wants to confirm a fact or experience. It also can be used to introduce a new topic, draw the listener's attention, and smoothly shift the conversation. Depending on the intonation and context, it can convey various nuances: a friendly, playful, or serious means of asking a question. Similar expressions include "그거 알아?" (Do you know that?) and "그거 기억나?" (Do you remember that?). Unlike the interrogative form "그거 알지?", 알지 (I know) conveys a sense of empathy or agreement with the speaker. Like 맞아 (that's right), it serves as an organic way of keeping the conversation flowing.

Action!

A 너 **그거 알지?** 다음 달에 데이식스 콘서트 있는 거.
You know, right? DAY6 is having a concert next month.

B 그럼 알지! 벌써 티켓 샀어.
Yeah, of course! I already bought my ticket.

A **그거 알지?** 내일부터 영화관 요금 오른대.
You know, right? Movie theater prices are going up starting tomorrow.

B 에이, 진짜? 몰랐어. 아 돈도 없는데 이제 집에서 유튜브나 봐야겠다.
No way, really? I had no idea. I'm broke. Guess I'll just watch YouTube at home now from now on.

A **그거 알아?** 우리 회사 앞에 카페 새로 문 열었더라.
You know right? A new cafe just opened in front of our office.

B 아~ 거기! 커피 맛있다던데.
Oh~ that place! I heard their coffee is really good.

33

내가 할게

I'll take care of it / I'll do it

〈너의 시간 속으로〉 (2023)

'내가 할게'를 사용할 수 있는 상황은?

In which situation would you use "내가 할게"?

ⓐ 책임을 피할 때

ⓑ 스스로 하겠다고 나설 때

ⓒ 다른 사람에게 강요할 때

Meaning & Use~

내가 할게 is used to express one's willingness or determination to take responsibility of something. It is primarily used in informal situations, and in actual day-to-day talk, 할게 is often omitted and 나! (Me!) or 내가! (I'll) is only said. Shortening it like this speeds up the conversation and, depending on the situation, can convey a higher degree of confidence or assertiveness. Especially in relationships where the context is well understood, the meaning can still be conveyed even when the verb is omitted. Similar expressions include "내가 맡을게." (I'll be responsible for it) or "내가 처리할게." (I'll complete it).

Action!

A 이번 프로젝트는 어떻게 하지?
How am I supposed to do with this project?

B ***내가 할게***. 걱정하지 마.
I'll take care of it. Don't worry.

A 누가 설거지할래? Who wants to do the dishes?

B ***내가***! Me!

A 웬일이냐, 해가 서쪽에서 뜨겠다.
What gives? That'll be the day.

A 가방 무거워 보이네. Your bag looks heavy.

B 괜찮아. It's okay.

A ***내가 들어 줄게***! I'll carry it for you!

34

MP3 034

그럴 거야

It most likely will... / Probably...

〈스타트업〉 (2020)

'그럴 거야'는 어떤 의미인가요?

What is the meaning of "그럴 거야"?

ⓐ 매우 확신함.

ⓑ 가능성을 추측함.

ⓒ 부정적인 태도를 보임.

Meaning & Use~

그럴 거야 is used to indicate possibility or express conjecture about a fact or situation. Even if it is uncertain, the speaker can use this expression to convey his/her belief or agreement. It is primarily used casually in everyday conversations, and the degree of certainty can be conveyed depending on the tone or intonation. When spoken with a soft intonation, it conveys a cautious guess; when spoken with a firm intonation, it can come across as a strong conviction. Variations include "아마 그럴 걸" (Probably so), "그럴 수도 있어" (It could be so), etc.

Action!

A 이번 주말에 비가 올 거라고 하던데.
I heard it's supposed to rain this weekend.

B ***그럴 거야***. 날씨가 흐리네.
Yeah, it most likely will. The sky looks cloudy.

A 너 내일 올 거지?
You're coming tomorrow, right?

B 응, ***그럴 거야***. 별일 없으면 갈게.
Yeah, I most likely will. Unless something comes up.

A 그 사람, 진짜 열심히 일하고 있더라.
That person is really working hard.

B 맞아, ***그럴 거야***. 정말 성실한 사람인 것 같았거든.
Yeah, he most likely will. He seems really dedicated.

35

MP3 035

뻔하지

I knew it / It's obvious

〈미지의 서울〉 (2025)

'뻔하지'는 어떤 상황에서 주로 사용되나요?

Which situations is "뻔하지" mainly used?

ⓐ 복잡한 문제를 설명할 때

ⓑ 새롭고 신기한 것을 말할 때

ⓒ 너무나 예상 가능한 것을 말할 때

뻔하지 is an expression that means something is obvious, its outcome or state is clear. It's used to describe predictable or self-evident situations, and is also commonly used to respond lightly to situations that are not surprising. Sometimes it's used to express criticism or disappointment, implying no further expectations or that the outcome is obvious and/or unsurprising. Depending on the intonation and context, it can convey various nuances: a playful agreement, indifference, or criticism. Variations of the expression include "뻔한 거 아니야?" (Isn't it obvious?), "뻔한 이야기야." (It's an obvious story.), "뻔한 레퍼토리야." (It's a predictable repertoire.), etc.

Action!

A 시험 공부 안 했지?
You didn't study for the test, did you?

B 이번엔 진짜 안 한 게 아니라 못 한 거야.
This time it's not that I didn't study, I just couldn't.

A **뻔하지.** 게임한다고 못한 거겠지.
I knew it. You probably couldn't because you were playing games.

A 걔 또 늦었어. He's late again.

B **뻔하지,** 뭐. I knew it though.

A 이 영화 결말이 너무 실망스러웠어.
The ending of this movie was so disappointing.

B 안 봐도 **뻔하지** 뭐.
I knew it without even watching it though.

36

MP3 036

장난 아니야

No joke / Seriously

〈왜 오수재인가〉 (2022)

'장난 아니야'는 어떤 감정을 표현할 때 사용할까요?

Which emotion would be expressed when using "장난 아니야"?

ⓐ 무관심

ⓑ 놀람과 감탄

ⓒ 짜증과 불만

Meaning & Use~

장난 아니야 is an expression meaning that something is exceptionally impressive, far exceeding the ordinary standard. Depending on the context and intonation, this phrase can convey various nuances: surprise and admiration at something impressive or outstanding, a phenomenon or situation that stands out, or the seriousness of a dangerous or uncomfortable situation. Therefore, it can convey both positive and negative meanings and is frequently used in everyday conversation when reacting to something that makes a lasting impression. Similar expressions include "진짜 대박이야," "장난 아닌데," etc.

Action!

A 어제 본 공연 어땠어?
How was the performance you saw yesterday?

B **장난 아니야.** 완전 감동적이었어.
No joke. It was totally moving.

A 저기 줄 좀 봐, 끝이 안 보여. 여기 진짜 맛집인가 봐.
Look at that line over there—it's endless. This place must be a real hot spot.

B 그러니까, 진짜 **장난 아니다.**
Exactly. No joke, really.

A 오늘 날씨 너무 덥지 않아?
Isn't it crazy hot today?

B **장난 아니야.** 밖에 5분만 있어도 쓰러질 것 같아.
No joke. I feel like I'd pass out after just five minutes outside.

37

MP3 037

뭐 하자는 거야?

What are you trying to do?

〈스물다섯 스물하나〉 (2022)

'뭐 하자는 거야?'는 언제 사용할까요?

When would you use "뭐 하자는 거야"?

ⓐ 칭찬할 때

ⓑ 혼란스러울 때

ⓒ 상대방을 격려할 때

뭐 하자는 거야? is an expression used when you feel someone else is displaying a challenging or hostile attitude, or when their words or actions are inappropriate for the situation, leading to conflict or tension. It primarily conveys dissatisfaction, protest, or warning, and depending on the intonation, it can range from a curious tone to an irritated response. Similar expressions include 왜 이래? (What's with you?), 무슨 의도야? (What's your intention?), etc.
Note that "뭐 하는 거야?" (What are you doing?) is mainly used when someone else is behaving in a way that is difficult to understand, while "뭐 하자는 거야?" (What are you trying to do?) is more frequently used when you feel they are displaying a challenging or hostile attitude toward you.

A 갑자기 시영이가 문을 잠갔어.
Siyoung suddenly locked the door.

B 대체 ***뭐 하자는 거야?***
What on earth is she trying to do?

연인과 심하게 다투는 상황
In the middle of a heated argument with her boyfriend

A 너 지금 나한테 거짓말하는 거지?
You're lying to me right now, aren't you?

B 나 진짜 피곤하다고. 그냥 다음에 얘기하자.
I'm tired, seriously. Let's just talk about it later.

A ***뭐 하자는 거야?*** 솔직하게 말하는 게 그렇게 힘들어?
What are you trying to do? Is it that hard for you to be honest?

A ***뭐 하는 거야?*** 왜 물건을 여기저기 다 흩어 놨어?
What are you trying to do? Why did you scatter things around everywhere?

B 너무 지저분해서 정리하려고 한 건데….
I tried to tidy up since it was messy....

A 더 어지럽잖아!
It's even messier now!

38

그만해

That's enough / Stop it

〈엄마친구아들〉 (2024)

'그만해'는 어떤 상황에서 사용할까요?

In which situation would you use "그만해"?

ⓐ 칭찬을 받을 때

ⓑ 재미있는 대화를 할 때

ⓒ 상대방의 행동을 멈추고 싶을 때

그만해 is the imperative form of 그만하다, meaning to stop or discontinue an action. It is a direct way of telling someone to stop an action or halt unpleasant or inappropriate behavior. It is frequently used in informal situations to express discomfort, vent annoyance, or give a warning. Similar expressions include "그만둬," "멈춰," etc.

Action!

A 야, **그만해**. 집중이 안 돼. Hey, stop it. I can't concentrate.

B 아…. 다리가 너무 저려서 계속 의자를 건드리게 되네. 미안.
Ah…. my leg is so numb that I keep bumping into your chair. Sorry.

A 네가 잘못했잖아! 인정해!
You're the one who messed up! Admit it!

B 아니, 전혀! 너나 잘해!
No, not at all! Take care of your own business.

C 둘 다 **그만해**. 이렇게 싸운다고 해결 안 돼.
Stop it, the both of you. Fighting like this won't solve anything.

A *(상대방을 계속 비꼬고 놀리며)* 너 진짜 이런 것도 몰라? 와, 대단하다~.
(Continues to mock and tease the other person) You seriously don't even know this? Wow, impressive~.

B **그만해**. 지금 농담으로 안 들려.
Stop it. That doesn't come across as a joke right now.

39

MP3 039

당장

Right away / Immediately

〈갯마을 차차차〉 (2021)

'당장'은 어떤 상황에서 사용할까요?

In which situation would you use "당장"?

ⓐ 상황을 무시할 때

ⓑ 천천히 행동하라고 할 때

ⓒ 지금 바로 행동해야 할 때

Meaning & Use~

당장 is an adverb meaning "without delay, immediately." It is used to demand immediate action and is frequently used in situations that emphasize urgency or immediacy. It is especially common when directing commands or instructions to someone. Depending on the context, it can come across as an urge, warning, or state of desperation. Similar expressions include 지금 바로 (Immediately, right now), 즉시 (on the spot), etc.

Action!

A 방이 너무 지저분하네. This room is way too messy.

B 네, 조금 있다가 치울게요. Yeah, I'll clean it up in a bit.

A 아니, **당장** 치워. No, clean it up right away.

A 그 위험한 기계 만지면 안 돼.
Don't touch that dangerous machine.

B 왜요? Why?

A **당장** 손 치워! 다칠 수도 있어.
Get your hands off it right now! You could get hurt.

A 보고서는 내일까지 준비하면 되죠?
The report can be ready by tomorrow, right?

B 아니, **당장** 보내야 해. 오늘 마감이야.
No, it has to be sent right now. The deadline is today.

MP3 040

왜 그래?

What's the matter with you?

〈호텔 델루나〉 (2019)

'왜 그래?'는 어떤 상황에서 주로 사용되나요?

In which situation would you mainly use "왜 그래?"?

ⓐ 새로운 정보를 질문할 때

ⓑ 상대방을 칭찬하고 싶을 때

ⓒ 상대방의 행동이 이상하거나 이해가 안 될 때

왜 그래? is a question asking for the reason or cause. It is used to ask someone about the reason for their behavior when it seems unusual, unexpected, or worrisome. Primarily used in casual contexts to question another person's attitude or actions. Depending on the tone and intonation, it can convey various emotions: surprise, dissatisfaction, or concern. Similar expressions include "왜 이래?" (What's wrong?), "무슨 일이야?" (What's up?), etc.

Action!

A *(이메일을 읽은 후)* 아 진짜 사람 열 받게 하네!

(After reading the email) Man, this is so infuriating!

B **왜 그래?** 무슨 문제 있어?

What's the matter with you? Do you have a problem?

A *(회의 도중 계속 핸드폰을 보며 딴청하는 김대리에게)*

김 대리 요즘 **왜 그래?** 집중 좀 해!!!

(To manager Kim, who keeps checking his phone and zoning out during the meeting) What's the matter with you recently? Focus, will you!!!

B 죄송합니다. 거래처 김 사장님 문자라서 바로 답변드리느라….

Sorry. I received a text from Mr. Kim, our client, so I had to reply right away....

A *(기운 없이 앉아 있는 친구에게 다가가서)* **왜 그래?** 무슨 일 있어?

(Approaching a friend sitting without energy) What's the matter with you? Did something happen?

B 오늘 알바 잘렸어. 매출이 떨어져서 알바생을 줄여야 한대.

I got fired from my part-time job today. Sales dropped, so they had to cut back on part-timers.

MP3 041

이게 뭐야?

What's this?

〈스타트업〉 (2020)

'이게 뭐야?'가 사용될 수 있는 상황을 모두 고르세요.

Choose all the situations in which "이게 뭐야?" can be used.

ⓐ 뭔가 마음에 안 들 때

ⓑ 새로운 것에 놀랐을 때

ⓒ 상대방의 말을 정확히 이해했을 때

Meaning & Use~

이게 뭐야? is an expression used to ask what something is. It is used to express curiosity, surprise, or dissatisfaction about something. It can also be used to express dissatisfaction with a situation that has already occurred and is not to one's liking. It is frequently used when something unexpected happens or when one is unsure of what something is. Similar expressions include "이게 도대체 뭐야?" (What in the world is this?), "뭐지?" (What's this?), etc.

Action!

A *(상자가 배달 온 것을 보고)* **이게 뭐야?** 내가 주문한 거 아니잖아.
(Seeing the box delivered) What's this? I didn't order anything.

B 아, 그거 네 생일 선물이야.
Oh, that's your birthday present.

A *(책상 위가 어질러진 걸 보고)* **이게 뭐야?** 이렇게 지저분하게 해 놓으면 어떡해.
(Seeing the messy desk) What's this? How can you leave things in such a messy state?

B 미안, 청소하려다가 급하게 나갔어.
Sorry, I was in the middle of cleaning but had to rush out.

A *(하늘에서 갑자기 폭죽이 터지자)* **이게 뭐야?** 오늘 무슨 날이야?
(Firecrackers suddenly go off in the sky) What's this? Is today a special day?

B 광복절이잖아. 몰랐어?
It's the Liberation Day. Didn't you know?

42

MP3 042

됐어

It's fine / Forget it

〈엄마친구아들〉 (2024)

'됐어'는 어떤 감정을 표현할 때 사용할까요?

Which emotion would be expressed when using "됐어"?

ⓐ 슬픔

ⓑ 포기나 실망

ⓒ 기쁨과 희망

돼어 is a phrase that indicates giving up or that something is no longer needed. In other words, it is used to express a lack of further interest or to give up on a certain matter or situation. It is also used when speaking in a tone that is dismissive or rejecting in nature. Depending on the tone and intonation, it can convey various nuances that range from a gentle refusal to dismissal. Similar expressions include "이제 됐어" (That's enough for now), "그만 얘기해" (Stop talking about it), etc.

Action!

A 이거 새로운 게임인데 해 볼래?
This is a new game. Wanna try it?

B **됐어**. 게임에는 관심 없어.
It's fine. I'm not into games.

A *(방금 찍은 핸드폰 사진을 들여다 보며)* 사진 잘 찍혔어?
(Looking at the photo just taken on the phone) Did the photo come out well?

B 아… 다 흔들렸네. **됐어**, 그냥 다음에 찍자.
Oh... it's all blurry. It's fine. Let's just take one next time.

A 내가 대신 해 줄게. I'll do instead.

B **됐어**. 내가 할게. It's fine. I'll do it.

A 내가 대신 가 줄게. 너 어제부터 허리 아프다고 했잖아.
I'll go for you instead. You said your back has been hurting since yesterday.

B **됐어**, 그래도 편의점은 나 혼자서 다녀올 수 있어.
It's okay. I can still go to the convenience store by myself.

43

MP3 043

알았어

Okay / I got it

〈나의 완벽한 비서〉 (2025)

'알았어'는 어떤 상황에서 주로 사용되나요?

In which situation would you mainly use "알았어"?

ⓐ 동의를 표현할 때

ⓑ 부탁을 거절할 때

ⓒ 놀라움을 표현할 때

Meaning & Use~

알았어 is a phrase that conveys understanding or acknowledgment. It is used casually to agree or confirm understanding, and is one of the most frequently used responses in everyday conversation. When someone else continues to do something despite telling them multiple times that you understand or acknowledge what they said, you can respond in a stronger tone by saying "알겠다고!" (I said I got it!). Similar expressions include "응, 알았어." (Yeah, got it), "이해했어." (I understood), etc.

A 내일 아침 일찍 와.
Come early tomorrow morning.

B **알았어**. 일어나는 대로 올게.
Got it. I'll come as soon as I wake up.

A 회의는 오후 3시에 시작합니다.
The meeting starts at 3 PM.

B 잘 **알겠습니다**. 확인해 주셔서 감사합니다.
I got it. Thank you for confirming.

A 잊지 말고 꼭 가져와야 해. 알았지?
Don't forget to bring it. Got it?

B **알았어**, 알겠다고! 몇 번을 말해.
Got it. I said I got it! How many times do I have to tell you?

MP3 044

너무해(요)

That is too much/so mean/unfair

〈킹더랜드〉 (2023)

'너무해'는 주로 어떤 감정을 표현할 때 사용되나요?

Which emotion would mainly be expressed when using "너무해"?

ⓐ 기쁠 때

ⓑ 이해가 안 될 때

ⓒ 상대방이 과하게 무언가를 요구할 때

Meaning & Use~

너무해 is an expression meaning "went too far." It can be used as a light complaint or in playful situations when someone else's actions or words feel unfair, or when the extent is deemed excessive to the extent of being too far. Depending on the tone and intonation, it can convey a range of emotions that range from cute whining to serious criticism. Similar expressions include "진짜 너무해." (Seriously, that's too much), "너무 심해." (That's way too much), etc.

Action!

A *(케이크를 혼자 다 먹고)* 아, 미안, 배고파서….

(After eating the whole cake alone) Oh, sorry, I was hungry....

B ***너무해***~ 난 한 입도 못 먹었는데….

That's so mean~ I didn't get a single bite....

A 사장님 오늘 일은 다 나한테만 시키시네.

Boss is making me do all the work today.

B 그러게, ***너무하시네***. 직원이 너 혼자만 있는 것도 아닌데 왜 저러시는 거지?

Yeah, that's really unfair. You're not the only employee here, why is he doing this?

A 네가 잘못해 놓고 그렇게 큰소리를 치면 어떡해.

How can you yell like that when you're the one who messed up?

B 그래도 ***너무해***. 그렇게까지 말할 건 아니잖아.

Still, it's unfair. He didn't need to say it like that.

MP3 045

신경 쓰지 마

Don't worry about it

〈여신강림〉 (2020~2021)

'신경 쓰지 마'는 어떤 상황에서 주로 사용되나요?

In which situation would you mainly use "신경 쓰지 마"?

ⓐ 놀랄 때

ⓑ 화가 날 때

ⓒ 상대방을 안심시킬 때

Meaning & Use~

신경 쓰지 마 is an expression that means there's no need to stress about every minor detail. It's used to tell someone not to fret or to stop overthinking about something. It's primarily used in friendly or informal conversations and, depending on the situation, can convey comfort or consideration. Similar expressions include "걱정하지 마." (Don't worry), "별거 아니야." (It's nothing), etc.

Action!

A 미안해. 내가 실수했어. Sorry. I messed up.

B 괜찮아. **신경 쓰지 마.** It's okay. Don't worry about it.

A 도와줘서 고마워! Thanks for helping me out!

B 에이, **신경 쓰지 마.** Oh, don't worry about it.

A 내가 오늘 하루 종일 너무 혼자 떠들었지? 미안해.
I talked to myself way too much today, didn't I? Sorry.

B 아니야. **신경 쓰지 마.**
No. Don't worry about it.

A 어제 언니한테 말실수를 했는데 그게 자꾸 생각나.
I said the wrong thing to my sister yesterday, and I can't stop thinking about it.

B 너무 **신경 쓰지 마.** 오늘 사과하면 되지.
Don't worry too much about it. You can apologize today.

46

-지 뭐

Happens though

〈스물다섯 스물하나〉 (2022)

해야 할 일이 아직 남아 있지만, 너무 피곤해서 더 이상 일을 할 수 없을 것 같은 기분이 듭니다. 이때 보일 수 있는 반응으로 알맞은 것은 무엇일까요?

There's work that still needs to be addressed, but you feel so tired that you can't do anything more. What would be an appropriate response in this situation?

ⓐ 끝까지 힘내서 하지 뭐.

ⓑ 친구들이랑 놀러 가지 뭐.

ⓒ 오늘은 이만 자러 가지 뭐.

-지 뭐 is an expression used to shrug off or accept a situation. Its meaning can vary depending on the context and tone. For instance, it can be naturally used when accepting something reluctantly without making an issue of it, when comforting or encouraging someone else, when calmly accepting a situation that was already anticipated, or when expressing regret about an outcome. Depending on the subject, tense, and honorific, different meanings can be conveyed. For example, when using the first or third person, acceptance is conveyed. On the other hand, when speaking in the second person, the impression of a suggestion, recommendation, and command is relayed. In honorific expressions, combining it with -시- sounds awkward or mocking. Therefore, rather than honorific politeness, an expression like "하시지요 뭐." (Why don't you do it?) emphasizes surprise or unexpectedness.

Action!

A 우리 가려던 식당이 문 닫았대. 내가 예약했어야 했는데 깜빡했어.
The restaurant we were going to go to is closed. I should've made a reservation but I forgot.

B 에이, 그런 날도 있**지 뭐**. 근처에 맛집 또 있잖아, 다른 데 가 보자.
Oh well, it happens. There are other good places nearby, let's try somewhere else.

A 내가 잠깐 등을 돌린 사이에 아이가 일어서다가 넘어져서 다쳤어. 한시도 눈을 떼지 말았어야 했는데.
While I turned my back for just a moment, the child stood up, fell, and got hurt. I should never have taken my eyes off her for a second.

B 아이를 키우다 보면 그럴 수도 있**지 뭐**. 작은 상처 하나 없이 키우는 건 불가능한 일이야. 너무 자책하지 마.
Stuff like that happens when you raise kids. It's impossible to raise them without them getting hurt. Don't be too hard on yourself.

A 지난 주말에 본 영화 정말 끔찍했어. 기대를 너무 많이 했나 봐.
That movie I saw last weekend was awful. I guess I had too high expectations.

B 그 감독 영화가 다 그렇**지 뭐**. 독특한 스타일이긴 하지만 호불호가 갈리잖아.
It happens though with that director's movies. He has a unique style, but you either love it or hate it.

A 다음엔 평점 높은 영화만 골라 봐야겠다.
Next time I'll only pick a movie with good reviews.

47

MP3 047

대충

Roughly / More or less

〈미지의 서울〉 (2025)

Quiz !?

'대충'은 어떤 상황에서 주로 사용되나요?

In which situation would you mainly use “대충”?

ⓐ 대강 처리할 때

ⓑ 완벽하게 계획할 때

ⓒ 세심하게 처리할 때

대충 is an expression meaning "to do something roughly or without precision." It is used when handling something quickly rather than aiming for a perfect result due to lack of time or because it is inconvenient. Similar expressions include 어림잡아 (rough estimate) and 대강 (roughly).

Action!

A 이 일을 어떻게 벌써 다 끝냈어?
How did you finish this already?

B 그냥 **대충** 했어.
I just more or less completed it.

A 회의가 언제 끝날 것 같아?
When do you think the meeting will end?

B 정확하진 않은데, **대충** 두 시간 정도 걸릴 것 같아.
I'm not sure exactly, but it'll take roughly about two hours.

A 그럼 그때 일정은 비워 두는 게 좋겠네.
Then I should probably keep my schedule open then.

A **대충** 계획은 세웠어?
Did you more or less plan it out?

B 응, 뭐 그런 대로. Yeah, sort of.

48

나도 그래

Same here / Me too

〈사랑의 이해〉 (2022)

'나도 그래'는 어떤 상황에서 주로 사용되나요?

In which situation would you mainly use "나도 그래"?

ⓐ 반대할 때

ⓑ 관심이 없을 때

ⓒ 동의를 표현할 때

나도 그래 is an expression meaning "I also feel the same." It's used when agreeing with someone or sharing the same feelings during a conversation. It can be shortened to "나도." (Me too) and is primarily used in friendly, informal conversations.

Action!

A 나 오늘 너무 피곤해. I'm so tired today.

B **나도 그래**. Same here.

A 이 영화 정말 재미있어. This movie is really interesting.

B **나도**! Me too!

A 여기 다음에 또 오고 싶어.
I want to come back here again next time.

B **나도 그래**. 또 같이 오자!
Same here. Let's come together again!

A 계획을 세워도 항상 그대로 되지는 않는 것 같아요.
Even when I make plans, things don't always go the way I expect.

B **나도 그래요**. 그래도 너무 스트레스 받지 않으려고 해요.
Me too. I try not to stress about it too much.

MP3 049

그냥

Just... / Simply...

〈도시남녀의 사랑법〉 (2020)

'그냥'이 사용될 수 있는 상황을 모두 고르세요.

Choose all the situations in which "그냥" can be used.

ⓐ 이유 없이 설명할 때

ⓑ 뭔가를 단순히 표현할 때

ⓒ 무언가를 특별하게 설명할 때

Meaning & Use~

그냥 is an expression meaning "without any particular reason or purpose." It is used when explaining something in a brief or natural manner, when indicating an action was taken without a special reason, when avoiding to give a reason, or when making a quick refusal. Especially in a situation following refusal, it serves as a somewhat buffer mechanism to imply only the bare minimum reason, politely block further questioning, and create distance (e.g., "됐어. 그냥 집에서 쉴래." (It's fine. I'll just rest at home.)). For example, it's used in phrases like "그냥 싫어." (I just don't like it) or "그냥 됐어." (Just let it be).

Action!

A 왜 거기 그러고 앉아 있어?
Why are you sitting over there like that?

B **그냥** 편해서. Just because; it's comfortable.

A 왜 그렇게 계속 웃고 있어?
Why are you smiling like that all the time?

B **그냥.** Just because.

A 싱겁긴…. How boring....

A 주말에 같이 여행 갈래?
Want to go traveling together this weekend?

B 됐어. **그냥** 집에서 쉴래.
I'm good. I'd rather just rest at home.

MP3 050

느낌이 이상해

Something feels off

〈오! 삼광빌라!〉 (2020~2021)

'느낌이 이상해'는 어떤 감정을 나타낼까요?

What emotion does "느낌이 이상해" exhibit?

ⓐ 피곤함

ⓑ 불안과 의심

ⓒ 행복과 기쁨

느낌이 이상해 is an expression meaning that one's bodily sensations or the energy/emotions perceived by oneself are not normal. It is used in everyday situations when feeling subtle discomfort or when a sense of unease is felt in the atmosphere. It is also used to express anxiety or caution about something dangerous or unfavorable that may arise. Depending on the tone and intonation, it can convey various nuances that from simple confusion to a firm warning. Similar expressions include "뭔가 이상해." (Something feels off), "분위기가 묘해." (The atmosphere is odd), or "느낌이 싸해." (I have a bad feeling about it). It is frequently combined with 뭔가 (something), which is an abbreviation for 무엇인가 (what) and is used to refer to an unspecified object or to express a state that is unclear but perceptible. Therefore, saying "뭔가 느낌이 이상해." (Something feels off) means that while the exact cause of the unease or discomfort cannot be pinpointed, there is an implicit feeling that something is off.

A 제니 오늘 말투가 왜 저래? 좀 이상하지 않아?
What's with Jenny's voice tone today? Doesn't it feel off?

B 응, 나도 ***느낌이 이상해***.
Yeah, I too sense that something feels off.

A 오늘 회식 자리 어땠어?
How was the company dinner tonight?

B 글쎄… 분위기는 좋았는데, 뭔가 ***느낌이 이상했어***.
Hmm... The vibe was good, but something just felt off.

A 이 골목으로 가면 더 빨리 갈 수 있어.
We can get there faster if we take this alley.

B 싫어, ***느낌이 이상해***. 다른 길로 가자.
I don't want to. Something feels off. Let's take another route.

Meaning & Use
Quiz !?
Action!

Action!
Part 2
말 습관 문형
Speech Patterns
Meaning & Use
Quiz !?

MP3 051

같은데

I think / It seems like...

흥, 긴장했네.

촌스럽게 방송 출연한다고
머리부터 발끝까지
잔뜩 힘주고 온 사람한테
들을 말은 아닌 것 **같은데요**.

〈킹더랜드〉 (2023)

'그 영화 재미있을 것 같은데.' 와 비슷한 표현이 아닌 것은?

Which is expression is not similar to "그 영화 재미있을 것 같은데."?

ⓐ 그 영화 재미있을 법하다.

ⓑ 그 영화 재미있을 듯 하다.

ⓒ 그 영화 재미있는 거 알아.

같- + -(으)ㄴ데 = 같은데

같은데 is a form that combines the adjective 같다 (to be similar) with the connecting suffix -(으)ㄴ데. It is used to convey, in a soft manner, the speaker's opinion, guess, impression, or memory. Here, -데 serves the function of making a suggestion or contrasting the former judgement or situation with what follows in the latter half of the sentence in a soft way. Therefore, 같은데 is often used when trying to avoid a definitive tone, when making a cautious guess, when sharing about uncertain memories, or when conveying information that naturally continues the conversation. Similar expressions include -(으)ㄹ 것 같다, -나 보다, -(으)ㄴ 가보다, -(으)ㄹ 듯하다, and -(으)ㄹ 법하다. For example, "문 닫을 시간인 것 같다." (It seems like its closing time) gently suggests the likelihood that it is closing time and naturally foreshadows that an explanation or suggestion will follow.

A 오늘 하늘이 좀 어두운 것 **같은데**, 비 올까?
The sky seems a little dark today. Is it going to rain?

B 응, 비가 올 것 같아. 우산 가져가는 게 좋겠어.
Yeah, it looks like it's going to rain. You'd better take an umbrella.

A 이 영화 정말 재미있는 것 **같은데**. 너는 어땠어?
This movie seems really fun. What did you think?

B 좋았어! 특히 결말이 인상적이었어.
It was good! The ending was especially impressive.

A 이번 프로젝트를 잘 마무리하지 못한 것 **같은데**, 넌 어떻게 생각해?
I don't think I finished this project well. What do you think?

B 나도 같은 생각이야. 다음번엔 또 실수하지 않도록 주의해야겠어.
Same here. We should be careful not to repeat the mistake next time.

A 지금 좀 바쁜 것 **같은데**, 나중에 만날까?
You seem a little busy right now. Shall we meet later?

B 그래, 저녁 시간에 만나자.
Okay, let's meet in the evening.

-(으)ㄹ걸?

I guess... / Probably...

〈선재 업고 튀어〉 (2024)

수업이 끝나고 교실에 돌아왔더니 친구가 보이지 않습니다. 다른 친구가 '벌써 집에 갔을걸?' 라고 말합니다. 이와 의미가 비슷하지 않은 문장은?

After class ended and I returned to the classroom, my friend was nowhere to be seen. Another friend said, "벌써 집에 갔을걸?". Which sentence does not have a similar meaning?

ⓐ 벌써 집에 갔대.

ⓑ 벌써 집에 갔겠지.

ⓒ 벌써 집에 갔을지도 몰라.

-(으) ㄹ + 거(것) + -ㄹ = -(으)ㄹ걸

-(으)ㄹ걸? is an expression used among close acquaintances when speculating or predicting something. It indicates that the speaker's guess differs from known facts or the listener's expectation, and can carry a meaning of light rebuttal or an exclamatory tone. Additionally, -(으)ㄹ걸? is the shortened version of -(으)ㄹ걸 그랬다 (should have done it), whereby 그랬다 is omitted. Depending on the context, it can also express mild regret or disappointment about something not done or a past situation. It uses the future tense ending -(으)ㄹ to indicate uncertainty, combines with 걸 to add a casual tone, and the intonation slightly raises at the end of the sentence when spoken. Similar expressions include -겠지, which indicates a stronger conjecture, and -나 봐 which serves as a natural, everyday assumption.

A 재현이는 왜 전화 안 받아?

Why isn't Jaehyun answering his phone?

B 아직 자고 **있을걸**? 어제 늦게까지 친구들이랑 모여서 놀았대.

He's probably still sleeping? I heard he was out late last night hanging out with friends.

A 어제 너무 늦게 잤어. 수업 발표 준비 하느라 잠을 못 잤어.

I went to bed way too late last night. I couldn't sleep because I was preparing for my class presentation.

B 준비를 그 정도로 열심히 했으면 발표 잘 **했겠는걸**?

If you worked that hard preparing, you probably did great on the presentation!

A 아, 좀 더 일찍 **나올걸**. 지금 가도 버스 이미 **떠났을걸**?

Oh, we probably should have arrived earlier. Even if we leave now, the bus would have probably already left.

B 아직 몰라. 우리 조금이라도 빨리 가 보자. 아직 안 왔을 수도 있잖아.

We won't know until we try. Let's try to go as quickly as we can. It might not have arrived yet.

53

MP3 053

-길래

As... / Because...

〈닥터 차정숙〉 (2023)

'비가 오길래 우산을 가져왔어'와 의미가 다른 문장은?

Which sentence has a different meaning from "비가 오길래 우산을 가져왔어"?

ⓐ 비가 와서 우산을 가져왔어.

ⓑ 비가 올 것 같아서 우산을 가져왔어.

ⓒ 비가 오는 것을 보고 우산을 가져왔어.

-길래

-길래 is a casual expression used to explain reasons based on 'personal evidence' that stem from directly seeing, hearing, or feeling a situation or sensation. Grammatically, it is the casual form of -기에, but its stronger subjective and experiential nuance makes it frequently used in natural everyday conversations. Compared to -아/어서 which conveys relatively objective reasons, -길래 gives off the impression that a certain action was taken after observing and judging a situation. It is attached to the stem of a verb or adjective, and to 이다, the stem of a verbal noun, or the endings -으시- and -었- between close acquaintances in everyday conversations.

Action!

A 아침에 왜 그렇게 서둘렀어? 무슨 일 있었어?
Why were you in such a hurry in the morning? What happened?

B 버스가 안 ***오길래*** 택시를 타고 왔어. 그래도 늦었지 뭐.
I took a taxi as the bus wasn't coming. Still ended up late, though.

A 다음엔 좀 더 여유 있게 나오는 게 좋겠네.
Next time, you should leave with a bit more time to spare.

A 무슨 ***일이길래*** 이렇게 시끄러운 거예요?
What's the commotion (as it sounds chaotic)?

B 이웃에서 불이 날 뻔했나 봐요. 소방차가 왔지만 큰불이 아니라 금방 꺼졌대요.
Looks like there almost was a fire at our neighbor's place. Fire trucks came, but it wasn't a big blaze and they put it out quickly.

A 너 왜 갑자기 집에 간 거야? 연락도 없이.
Why did you suddenly go home? Without even contacting me.

B 비가 엄청 ***오길래*** 그냥 일찍 들어갔어. 밖에 더 있으면 완전 다 젖을 것 같더라고.
I just went home as it started pouring. I figured if I stayed out longer, I'd get completely soaked.

-(으)ㄴ/는 거 아니야/ 아니에요?

MP3 054

Isn't this...? / Aren't you...?

〈이두나!〉 (2023)

당신은 버스 정류장에서 친구와 버스를 기다리고 있습니다. 하지만 버스가 떠났을까 봐 불안합니다. 어떻게 말하는 것이 가장 자연스러울까요?

You're waiting for the bus with a friend at the stop. But, you're anxious that the bus might have already left. Which one of the following expressions sounds most natural?

ⓐ 우리 버스 곧 올 거야.

ⓑ 우리 버스 이미 떠난 거 아니야?

ⓒ 우리 버스 아직 안 온 거 아니야?

-(으)ㄴ/는 + 거(것) + 아니- + -야 = -(으)ㄴ/는 거 아니야

-(으)ㄴ/는 거 아니야? is a colloquial expression used to request confirmation or suggest the possibility of something being the truth. It is often used to gently point out what the other person may have overlooked or to express doubt. For example, "이거 네가 한 거 아니야?" (Isn't this something you did?) could simply be a question seeking confirmation of a fact, but it can also carry a nuance of subtly challenging or playfully accusing the other person about their actions or words. Imagine a scene in a classroom where a student finds a desk in disarray and, glancing at a friend beside them with a playful smile, says, "이거 네가 한 거 아니야?" (Didn't you do this?). In such cases, the tone and expression can convey a light-hearted joke, friendly suspicion, or playful accusation. The polite form is -(으)ㄴ/는 거 아니에요?

서점에서 At the bookstore

A 이 책, 네가 지금 읽고 ***있는 거 아니야***?
Isn't this the book you're reading right now?

B 맞아, 선희가 추천해 줘서 정말 재미있게 읽고 있어.
Correct. Sunhee recommended it, and I'm really enjoying it.

A 이 그림, 고흐가 ***그린 거 아니에요***?
Isn't this painting by Van Gogh?

B 고갱 작품이에요. 고흐와 고갱은 이름이 비슷해서 자주 헷갈려요.
It's a piece by Gauguin's. Van Gogh and Gauguin have similar names, so I often get them mixed up.

A 왜 화병이 깨져 있지?
Why is the vase broken?

B 오늘 아침에 지수가 물 갈기로 했었잖아. 지수가 ***깬 거 아니야***?
Didn't Jisoo say she'd change the water this morning? Isn't Jisoo the one who broke it?

A 아니야. 점심 때까지 멀쩡하던 거 내가 확인했어.
No. I checked, and it was fine until lunchtime.

55

MP3 055

-더라고(요)

I noticed/realized...

〈힘쎈여자 강남순〉 (2023)

새로 생긴 카페를 방문해서 커피를 마셔 본 것에 대해 친구에게 이야기하고 싶습니다.
어떤 표현이 가장 자연스러울까요?

I want to tell my friend about visiting a new cafe and trying their coffee.
Which one of the following expressions sounds most natural?

ⓐ 커피가 정말 맛있더라고.

ⓑ 커피가 정말 맛있어 보이더라고.

ⓒ 커피가 정말 맛있을 것 같더라고.

-더라 + -고(요) = -더라고(요)

-더라고(요) is used when the speaker recalls and conveys a fact they personally experienced, witnessed, or realized in the past. For example, it conveys personal experience or an insight gained from observation, like "어제 정말 춥더라고." (I noticed it was really cold yesterday.). It is typically used when the speaker recounts an anecdote based on their own experience. As such, in such cases, it is not used in the first-person. However, the first-person can be used when expressing feelings, moods, or mental states. -더군(요) and -더라 serve similar functions.

Ⓐ 어제 소개팅은 어땠어?
How was your blind date yesterday?

Ⓑ 가로수길에 새로 생긴 카페가 인기가 많다고 해서 같이 갔는데, 분위기가 정말 **좋더라고**.
We went to this new cafe on Garosu-gil that's really popular, and I noticed that the atmosphere was amazing.

Ⓐ 정말? 나도 이번 주말에 가 봐야겠다.
Really? I should check that area out this weekend.

Ⓐ 태하가 직접 만든 케이크를 줬는데, 정말 **맛있더라고**. 특히 그 크림이 너무 부드러워서 먹을 때마다 행복했어.
Taeha gave me a cake he made himself, and I realized it was so delicious. Especially that cream—it was so smooth, every bite made me happy.

Ⓑ 오, 안 그래도 태하가 케이크를 진짜 잘 만든다고 들었어. 나도 태하한테 케이크 만드는 법 좀 알려 달라고 해야겠다.
Oh, I've heard Taeha is really good at making cakes. I should ask him to teach me how to make them too.

Ⓐ 저는 지난 주말에 템플 스테이를 갔다 왔어요.
I went for a temple stay last weekend.

Ⓑ 어땠어요? 저도 한 번 가 본 적 있는데, 오랜만에 평화로운 시간을 보낼 수 있어서 마음에 **들더라고요**.
How was it? I went once too, and I really liked it. I realized it was nice to have some peaceful time after so long.

56

MP3 056

-게 됐어

I ended up... / It turned out...

〈미생〉 (2014)

오늘 친구와 저녁을 먹을 계획이었지만, 예상치 못한 일이 생겨 취소해야 합니다. 어떻게 상황을 설명할까요?

You planned to have dinner with a friend tonight, but an unexpected event came up and you have to cancel. How would you explain the situation?

ⓐ 일이 생겨서 저녁을 먹었어.

ⓑ 일이 생겨서 저녁을 취소했어.

ⓒ 일이 생겨서 저녁을 같이 못 먹게 됐어.

-게 + **되-** + **-었-** + **-어** = **-게 됐어**

-게 됐어 indicates that, regardless of the speaker's intent, something happened due to external circumstances or the flow of events. Depending on the tone, it is often used to gently convey a situation and can convey that an unwanted event occurred. It is also used when a state has changed leading to a result, such as habits formed over time or shifts in preferences. Additionally, it can be used as a natural expression of a favorable outcome. For example, when something unexpected but positive has happened.

Action!

A 원래는 해외여행을 가려고 했는데, 일이 많아서 ***못 가게 됐어***.
I was planning to go on an overseas trip, but I ended up not being able to go because I had too much work to do.

B 아쉽다. 다음에 나랑 같이 가자!
That's too bad. Let's go together next time!

A 지인의 소개로 그 회사에 ***취직하게 됐어요***.
I ended up getting hired at that company through an acquaintance's referral.

B 정말 잘 됐네요! 축하합니다. 한턱내세요!
That's really great news! Congratulations. Treat us!

A 어제 보니 축구를 정말 잘하더라. 원래 축구를 좋아했어?
I noticed yesterday that you play soccer really well. Did you always like soccer?

B 원래는 별로 안 좋아했는데, 동생이 좋아해서 같이 하다 보니 나도 ***좋아하게 됐어***.
I didn't really like it at first, but my younger sibling likes soccer, so I started playing with him and ended up liking it too.

MP3 057

-잖아(요)

(I told you/You told me...) right?

〈선재 업고 튀어〉 (2024)

다음 중 불만을 표현하는 문장은?

Which one of the following sentences expresses dissatisfaction?

ⓐ 지금 공부하고 있잖아!

ⓑ 내일 영화 볼 거잖아. 무슨 영화 볼까?

ⓒ 어제 숙제하고 있었잖아, 어렵지 않았어?

-지 + 않- + -아(요) = -잖아(요)

-잖아(요) is used to remind someone else of a fact they already know or to emphasize a point. For example, in "오늘 쉬는 날이잖아." (It's your day off today, right?), 잖아 is used to highlight shared information or reconfirm something . It's also frequently used to point out or scold someone when negative consequences arise because they didn't listen despite warning them. When combined with -고 있다, it emphasizes that an action is currently in progress, serving to correct a situation or express frustration or dissatisfaction. For instance, "지금 보고 있잖아." emphasizes that the TV is already being watched, while "지금 준비하고 있잖아." reminds the listener that the action of making preparations has already begun. It is widely used in various contexts such as persuasion, explanation, and expressing dissatisfaction.

Action!

A 그 영화 재미없다고 ***했잖아***. 왜 봤어?
I told you that movie was boring, right? Why did you watch it?

B 그러게 말야. 그 시간에 상영하는 작품이 그것 밖에 없어서 어쩔 수 없었어.
Tell me about it. There was nothing else airing at that time, so I literally had no choice.

A 아, 어젯밤에 잠이 안 와서 혼났어. 너무 늦게 잤더니 피곤하네.
Ah, I couldn't sleep last night and almost died from fatigue. I went to bed super late and now I'm exhausted.

B 그러게 내가 저녁에는 커피 마시지 말라고 ***했잖아***.
See, I told you not to drink coffee in the evening, right?

A 앞으로는 진짜 조심해야겠다. 예전에는 밤에 커피 마시고도 잘 잤는데 말이야.
I really need to be careful from now on. In the past, I used to be able to sleep fine even after drinking coffee at night.

A 오늘 점심 어디서 먹을까?
Where should we eat lunch today?

B 우리 오늘 회식 ***있잖아***. 점심은 가볍게 먹어야 하지 않을까?
I told you that we have a company dinner tonight, right? Shouldn't we have a light lunch?

58

MP3 058

-고 말았어

I end(ed) up...

〈사랑의 불시착〉 (2019~2020)

'다이어트 중인데 결국 치킨을 먹고 말았어.' 와 비슷한 표현은?

What's a similar expression to "다이어트 중인데 결국 치킨을 먹고 말았어."?

ⓐ 결국 치킨을 먹어 버렸어.

ⓑ 결국 치킨을 먹어야 했어.

ⓒ 결국 치킨을 먹고 말 거야.

-고 + 말- + -았- + -어 = -고 말았어

-고 말았어 indicates that something happened regardless of the speaker's intention or will. It gives off the impression that feelings of regret, frustration, or resignation exist. This expression emphasizes the finality of an action, signifying an unexpected outcome or an undesired event occurring. It is primarily used with words like 결국 (in the end), 끝내 (finally), or 마침내 (at last) to highlight the result. However, it can also convey the meaning of achieving something difficult under challenging circumstances, as in "우리 팀이 계속 지다가 결국 이기고 말았어." (Our team kept losing but, in the end, ended up winning.). A strong determination to achieve something is often conveyed with the volitional marker -겠-, forming constructions like -고 말겠어. It attaches to verbs in the past tense and is not used with adjectives. It can be conjugated in both the first-person and third-person, as in "여자 친구와 헤어지고 말았어요." (I ended up breaking up with my girlfriend.) or "여자 친구가 저를 떠나고 말았어요." (My girlfriend ended up leaving me.). Adding -야 after -고 can add emphasis. For example, expressions like "기차가 떠나 버리고야 말았다." (The train ended up leaving).

A 다이어트 중인데도 결국 언니의 꼬임에 넘어가서 어제 맥주를 **마시고 말았어**.
I'm on a diet, but my sister persuaded me and I ended up drinking beer yesterday.

B 에이, 괜찮아. 한 번쯤은 괜찮지.
Your good. It's fine once in a while (to treat yourself to a beer).

A 오늘 잠들기 전에 이 단어들을 기필코 다 **외우고야 말겠어**!
Before I fall asleep tonight, I'm going to end up memorizing all these words!

B 너 너무 피곤해 보이는데 그러지 말고 오늘은 이만 자는 게 어때? 언어 공부는 꾸준히 하는 게 중요하지 한 번에 많이 하는 게 중요한 게 아니잖아.
You look so tired. Why not just go to bed now? Language learning is about consistent efforts, not cramming everything all at once.

A 버스를 놓치지 않으려고 뛰었는데, 결국 **놓치고 말았어요**.
I ran to catch the bus, but I ended up missing it in the end.

B 다음 버스가 금방 올 거예요. 너무 걱정하지 마세요.
The next bus will be here soon. Don't worry about it too much.

59

MP3 059

-는 중이야

I'm in the middle of... / On the way...

〈봄밤〉 (2019)

친구가 전화를 했을 때, 지금 저녁 식사 중이라고 말하려면 어떻게 표현할까요?

When a friend calls, how would you say that you are eating dinner at the moment?

ⓐ 방금 저녁을 먹었어.

ⓑ 지금 저녁을 먹을 거야.

ⓒ 지금 저녁을 먹는 중이야.

-는 + 중 + 이 + -야 = -(으)ㄴ/는 중이야

-는 중이야 is an expression that indicates an action is currently in progress. For example, the sentence "지금 숙제하는 중이야." (I'm doing my homework right now.) emphasizes an ongoing action (doing homework) and such an expression is primarily used in everyday conversations. It can also be used as a response when someone asks about the progress of a specific task. For instance, if someone asks, 는 어떻게 됐어? (How's ~ going?) or 는 어떻게 되어가고 있어? (How's ~ progressing?), replying by saying -는 중이야 implies that the task is not yet fully completed but is being handled without major issues. -는 중이에요 and -는 중입니다 can be used when speaking in the polite form.

A 예림아, 지금 뭐 해?

Yelim, what are you doing?

B ***요리하는 중이야***. 사실, 요즘 새로운 레시피를 시도해 보고 있는데, 오늘은 새우 파스타를 만들고 있어.

I'm in the middle of cooking. To be honest, I've been trying out new recipes lately, and today I'm making shrimp pasta.

A 와, 맛있겠다! 나도 파스타 좋아하는데. 나중에 어떻게 만들었는지 알려 줄래?

Wow, that sounds delicious! I love pasta too. Can you tell me how you made it later?

A 지난주에 얘기한 기획안은 어떻게 됐어요?

How's that proposal we talked about last week coming along?

B 네, 이제 기대 효과 부분 ***작성하는 중입니다***. 오늘 안으로 마무리할 수 있을 것 같습니다.

Yeah, I'm in the middle of working on the expected results section right now. I should be able to finish it today.

A 좋아, 내일 오전 회의 시간까지 문제 없이 끝내도록 하세요.

Sounds good. Make sure you complete it without any issues by tomorrow morning's meeting.

-나 봐

I guess… / It seems like…

〈도깨비〉 (2016~2017)

친구가 '왜 민지가 전화를 안 받아?'라고 물었을 때, 당신은 민지가 다른 일로 바쁘다고 생각합니다. 이때 어떤 표현을 사용할 수 있을까요?

Your friend asks "Why isn't Minji answering her phone?". You think Minji is busy doing something. Which one of the following expressions would you use in this situation?

ⓐ 민지가 지금 바쁜가 봐.

ⓑ 민지가 지금 전화 중이야.

ⓒ 민지가 지금 전화를 하고 싶어 해.

-나 + 보- + -아 = -나 봐

-나 봐 is a colloquial expression used when the speaker makes an assumption based on an observation, the surrounding circumstances, or some sort of clue. It is primarily attached after verbs or descriptive particles to infer present or past actions/situations. However, it can be used with adjectives: it changes to the form -ㄴ가 봐 when inferring the present state and -았/었나 봐 when inferring past situations or states. For example, "그 사람이 바쁜가 봐." (I guess that person is busy.) conveys a guess about the current state of someone else, while "어제 비가 왔나 봐." (I guess it rained yesterday.) indicates a guess about something that took place in the past. This expression reveals the speaker's judgment in a gentle manner and is frequently used in everyday conversations. It can also be used in a question-like way by raising the end of the expression. Polite forms include -나 봐요 or -나 봅니다.

Action!

A 왜 민지가 오늘 약속에 안 왔지?
Why didn't Minji come to the appointment today?

B ***바쁜가 봐***. 요즘 일이 많다고 했잖아.
I guess she's busy. She mentioned having a lot on her plate lately.

A 그래도. 말도 없이 안 올 친구가 아닌데. 무슨 일이 생긴 건 아닌지 걱정돼.
Still. She's not the type who cancels without a word. I'm worried something might have happened.

A 오늘 무슨 축제가 ***있나 봐***. 밖에 사람들이 많네.
I guess there's some kind of festival being held today. There are so many people outside.

B 아, 오늘 광안리 해수욕장에서 드론 쇼가 있다고 했어.
Oh, I heard there's a drone show at Gwangalli Beach today.

A 김 대리님, 요즘 기분이 좋아 보이죠?
Don't you think Mr. Kim seems to be in a good mood lately?

B 여자 친구가 ***생겼나 봐요***. 지난번에 우연히 데이트하는 모습을 봤어요.
I guess he got a girlfriend. I happened to see them on a date the other day.

MP3 061

-(으)ㄹ래?

Do you want to...?

〈도시남녀의 사랑법〉 (2020)

'차 한잔 할래?'는 어떤 의미일까요?

What does "차 한잔 할래?" mean?

ⓐ 차를 빨리 운전하라는 요청

ⓑ 차를 마시면서 쉬자는 제안

ⓒ 함께 차를 마시고 싶지 않다는 거절

-(으)ㄹ + -래 = -(으)ㄹ래?

-(으)ㄹ래? is used at the end of the sentence to express the speaker's intention to do something in the future or to ask about the other person's preference/intention. It is frequently used in an indirect way to express one's intention or to suggest an activity or plan among close acquaintances. As such, it is spoken in a gentle tone which gives off the impression of offering a choice rather than insistence. For a more polite form, use -(으)ㄹ래요?

Action!

A 오늘 저녁에 뭐 할 거야?
What are you doing tonight?

B 아무 계획 없는데. 같이 저녁 **먹을래**?
No plans. Shall we grab dinner together?

A 이번 주말에 놀이공원에 **갈래**?
Shall we go to the amusement park this weekend?

B 좋아! 우리 고등학교 때 교복도 입고 가자! 다른 친구들이 교복 입고 가서 찍은 사진 보니까 예쁘더라.
Sounds good! Let's wear our high school uniforms too! I saw pictures other friends took wearing theirs, and it looked pretty.

A 교복이 아직 집에 있는지 모르겠네. 오늘 집에 가서 한번 찾아볼게.
I'm not sure if I still have my uniform at home. I'll look for it when I get home today.

A 오늘 날씨 너무 좋다. **산책할래**?
The weather's so nice today. Shall we go for a walk?

B 그래, 오랜만에 공원 한 바퀴 돌자. 요즘 계속 실내에만 있어서 답답했잖아.
Yeah, let's take a stroll around the park. It's been ages. It's been so stifling since we've only been indoors lately, right?

62

MP3 062

-(으)ㄴ/는 것 같아

It seems like... / I think...

〈선재 업고 튀어〉 (2024)

친구와 저녁 늦게 카페에 갔습니다. 카페 안에 사람이 한 명도 없어서 친구가 '왜 이렇게 조용해?'라고 물어봤어요. 어떤 답이 가장 자연스러울까요?

You went to a cafe late at night with a friend. There wasn't a single person inside, so your friend asks, "Why is it so quiet?".

ⓐ 비가 온 것 같아.

ⓑ 사람들이 올 것 같아.

ⓒ 문 닫을 시간인 것 같아.

-(으)ㄴ + 것 + 같- + -아 = -(으)ㄴ/는 것 같아

-(으)ㄴ/는 것 같아 is used to gently convey the speaker's opinion, guess, impression, or recollection. -(으)ㄴ/는 것 같아 is used when speaking of present or future situations and -았/었던 것 같아 is used when recalling past situations or experiences. Because it conveys a nuance of leaving possibilities open rather than stating something definitively, it is frequently used when politely declining a request or favor. It is often used to politely decline a request or favor, to make a cautious guess, or to express uncertain memories, as in "그건 좀 어려울 것 같아." (It seems like that might be difficult.) or "시간이 안 될 것 같아." (It seems like I won't have time.). When using it in the past tense, it not only conveys a simple recollection but also vividly recounts the past by bringing together various actions or states. For example, "그때 정말 행복했던 것 같아." (It seems like I was really happy back then.) is an expression that brings back feelings, impressions, or emotions that were felt in the past.

Action!

A 작년보다 올해 겨울이 더 ***추운 것 같아***.
It seems like this winter is colder than last year.

B 그것도 지구 온난화의 영향 중 하나래. 여름은 점점 더 더워지고,
겨울은 점점 더 추워지는 거지.
They say that's also one of the effects of global warming.
Summers are getting hotter and winters are getting colder.

A 이 문제 답이 뭐야?
What's the answer to this question?

B 내 생각엔 ***3번인 것 같아***.
It seems like number 3 to me.

A 작년에 교환 학생 갔다 왔다고 했었지? 어땠어?
You said you went on an exchange program last year, right? How was it?

B 그때가 내 인생 최고의 ***날들이었던 것 같아***.
It seems those were the best days of my life.

MP3 063

-게

So that...

〈스물다섯 스물하나〉 (2022)

'잘 보이게 여기에 놓아.'는 어떤 의미일까요?

What does "잘 보이게 여기에 놓아." mean?

ⓐ 잘 보이는지 확인한다.

ⓑ 잘 보이게 하는 방법을 묻는다.

ⓒ 잘 보일 수 있도록 여기에 놓는다.

-게

-게 is used to indicate the purpose or intention behind an action. By attaching -게 to the verb stem, it explains the reason or goal for performing a certain action. For example, "사람들한테 잘 보이게 문 옆에 붙이자." (Let's put it next to the door so that people can see it well.) indicates the reason for placing the sign next to the door is "to make it visible to people." Similarly, "사람들이 이야기할 수 있게" (so that people can talk) expresses the purpose of lowering the music in order to enable people to have conversations. Thus, -게 can function as an object clause in the middle of a sentence or emphasize the reason or goal at the end of a sentence.

Action!

A 간판을 어디에 붙일까?
Where should we put the sign?

B 사람들한테 잘 ***보이게*** 문 옆에 붙이자.
Let's put it next to the door so people can see it well.

A 음악 좀 작게 틀어 줄래? 사람들이 이야기할 수 ***있게***.
Can you turn the music down? So that people can talk.

B 아, 맞아. 너무 시끄러우면 대화하기 힘들지.
Oh, right. It's hard to have a conversation when it's too loud.

A 회의 자료는 어떻게 배치할까?
How should we arrange the meeting materials?

B 자리마다 한 부씩 미리 올려 두자. 모두 도착하면 바로 확인할 수 ***있게***.
Let's place one copy at each seat ahead of time, so everyone can check it as soon as they arrive.

-(으)ㄹ 뻔했어

I almost (didn't, couldn't, etc)...

〈선재 업고 튀어〉 (2024)

다음 중 누군가가 '넘어질 뻔했어.'라고 말했을 때, 무슨 일이 있었는지 가장 잘 설명하는 것은 무엇인가요?

Which one of the following best describes what happened when someone said, "넘어질 뻔했어."?

ⓐ 확실히 넘어졌다

ⓑ 넘어지지 않았고, 넘어질 가능성도 없었다

ⓒ 거의 넘어질 것 같았지만 넘어지지 않았다

-(으)ㄹ + 뻔하- + -았- + -어 = -(으)ㄹ 뻔했어

-(으)ㄹ 뻔했어 is used when, up until just a moment ago, what was about to happen seemed clearly predictable but ultimately did not occur. For example, 넘어질 뻔했어 means one was on the verge of falling but ultimately did not. It's often used when narrowly escaping an unexpected event or dangerous moment, conveying a nuance of surprise or relief. 간 떨어질 뻔하다 (literally, "my liver almost fell out") is an idiomatic expression that has a similar meaning to "you scared the life out of me" and is used when experiencing a startling moment.

Action!

A 뭘 하고 있었길래 내가 뒤에서 살짝 다가온 것도 눈치 못 채?

What were you doing that you didn't even notice me sneak up behind you?

B 깜짝이야! 간 ***떨어질 뻔했잖아***.

What the heck! You scared the life out of me.

A 왜 이렇게 헐떡거려?

Why are you panting like that?

B 버스에서 넷플릭스를 보다가 못 ***내릴 뻔했어***. 문이 닫히기 직전에 겨우 내렸네.

I was watching Netflix on the bus and almost missed my stop. I got off just as the door was closing.

A 시험 어땠어?

How was the exam?

B ***망칠 뻔했는데***, 마지막 배점 높은 문제를 맞혀서 다행히 합격한 것 같아.

I almost messed up, but luckily I got the last high-point question right, so I think I passed.

65

-(으)ㄹ 테니까

So... / Since...

〈선재 업고 튀어〉 (2024)

'내가 책임지고 해결할 테니까 걱정하지 마!'의 의미와 가장 잘 맞는 문장은 무엇일까요?

Which sentence best matches the meaning of "내가 책임지고 해결할 테니까 걱정하지 마!"?

ⓐ 네가 책임져야 내가 걱정 안 해.

ⓑ 내가 이미 해결했으니 걱정할 필요 없어.

ⓒ 내가 알아서 처리할게, 그러니 마음 놓아도 돼.

-(으)ㄹ + 터 + 이 + -니까 = -(으)ㄹ 테니까

-(으)ㄹ 테니까 expresses the speaker's intention, conjecture, or advice, with the first half of the sentence serving as the reason or basis for the latter half of the sentence. 테 (터 + 이) indicates the speaker's strong intention or conviction, while -니까 indicates the reason. For example, "내가 도울 테니까 걱정하지 마." (I'll help, so don't worry) conveys the meaning "Since I will help, you should not worry." It is primarily used to reassure someone or to propose and explain a plan. Grammatically, if the verb stem ends in a vowel, -ㄹ is added; if it ends in a consonant, -을 is added, followed by 테니까.

Action!

A 비가 올 것 같아. 우산 안 가져왔는데….
It looks like it's going to rain. But, I didn't bring an umbrella....

B 우리 동생이 곧 우산을 ***가져올 테니까*** 그거 같이 쓰자.
My younger sibling will bring one soon, so let's share it.

A 저희 팀플 역할 분담을 어떻게 할까요?
How should we divide the roles for our group project?

B 제가 자료 조사를 ***해 올 테니까***, 발표를 맡아 주실래요?
I'll be in charge of researching the sources, and how about you present (the presentation)?

A 선생님, 이거 너무 어려워서 못 풀겠어요.
Teacher, this is too hard that I can't solve it.

B 지난주에도 설명해 준 개념이잖아. 마지막으로 한 번만 더 ***설명할 테니까*** 이번엔 잘 들어.
I explained this concept last week, right? I'll explain it one last time, so listen attentively this time.

MP3 066

-(으)ㄹ지도 몰라

It might be... / I don't know, maybe...

사실 수의사님 코칭
틀린 건 **아닐지도 몰라요.**
있다 없어지는 것만큼
신경 쓰이는 일도 없으니까.

〈어쩌다 전원일기〉 (2022)

누군가 '비가 올지도 몰라.'라고 말했습니다. 이 말을 들었을 때, 다음 이어질 말로 가장 적절한 것은 무엇인가요?

Someone tells you, "비가 올지도 몰라." When you hear this, which one of the following is the most appropriate response?

ⓐ 혹시 모르니 우산을 챙기세요.

ⓑ 아직 날씨가 맑으니까 무시하세요.

ⓒ 이미 비가 오고 있으니 집에 있으세요.

-(으)ㄹ + 지 + 도 + 모르- + -아 = -(으)ㄹ지도 몰라

-(으)ㄹ지도 몰라 is used when the speaker acknowledges uncertainty while leaving open the possibility that something may happen. It's effective for avoiding a direct straight-forward response, while getting the message across in a gentle manner. After verb or adjective stems, it combines with the future form -(으)ㄹ to form expressions like "갈지도 몰라" (I might go) or "추울지도 몰라" (It might be cold). When combined with nouns, it uses the future form of the predicate particle 이다 (to be), as in "학생일지도 몰라" (He/she might be a student). While it primarily indicates possibility in the present or future tenses, it can also be used in the past tense to express conjecture about past events. For example, "왔을지도 몰라" (He/she might have come).

A 오늘 소풍 갈 수 있을까?
Do you think we can go on the picnic today?

B 날씨가 흐린 걸 보니 비가 ***올지도 몰라***. 다음 주로 미루는 거 어때?
The weather is cloudy, so it might rain. How about we postpone it to next week?

A 볼펜을 떨어뜨렸어. 이건 시험에 떨어지게 될 거라는 의미야. 나 이제 어떡해?
I dropped my pen. This is a sign that I'll fail the test. What am I going to do now?

B 반대로 생각해 봐. 볼펜이 떨어진 게 아니라 바닥에 붙은 거지. 네가 시험에 붙을 거라는 ***의미일지도 몰라***.
Think about it in another way. The pen didn't fall; instead, it stuck to the floor. It might mean that you'll pass the test.

A 길이 막힐까? Do you think there will be traffic?

B 주말이라서 좀 ***막힐지도 몰라***.
It's the weekend, so there might be a traffic jam.

67

MP3 067

-기만 하면

Whenever... / As long as...

〈폭싹 속았수다〉 (2025)

시험을 앞두고 걱정하는 친구에게 '열심히 공부하기만 하면 걱정할 필요 없어.'라고 말했습니다. 이 말이 의미하는 것은 무엇일까요?

You told your friend who is worried before an exam, "열심히 공부하기만 하면 걱정할 필요 없어." What does this mean?

ⓐ 열심히 하는 것만이 성공의 조건이다

ⓑ 열심히 하지 않아도 성공이 보장된다

ⓒ 열심히 하는 것과 성공은 아무 상관이 없다

-기 + 만 + 하- + -면 = -기만 하면

-기만 하면 is used to express a condition which emphasizes a single condition that decisively affects the outcome among multiple conditions. For example, "시간을 맞추기만 하면 돼." means"All is good as long as you are accountable of the time." It is also used to emphasize that a specific condition always leads to the same result that occurs repeatedly. For example, "두 사람은 만나기만 하면 싸운다" means "whenever the two meet, a fight inevitably breaks out."

A 시험 잘 볼 수 있을까?
Will I be able to do well on the exam?

B 열심히 ***공부하기만 하면*** 걱정할 필요 없어.
There's no need to worry as long as you study hard.

A 어휴, 두 사람 또 싸우네. 매번 싸우는 거 지겹지도 않나?
Ugh, those two are at it again. Don't they ever get tired of fighting all the time?

B 둘이 ***만나기만 하면*** 싸우는 거 알면서 왜 같이 불렀어?
You know they fight whenever they meet, so why did you invite them both?

A 이제 나이도 들고 했으니까 철이 들었을 줄 알았지.
Now that they're older, I thought they matured.

A 이번 모임 장소는 어디로 할까? 좋은 아이디어 있는 사람?
Where should we meet this time? Any good ideas?

B 나는 지하철역에서 ***가깝기만 하면*** 돼. 너무 더워서 오래 걷고 싶지 않아.
I'm good with anywhere as long as it is close to a subway station. I don't want to walk long distances since it is so hot.

MP3 068

68

-았/었으면 좋겠어

I wish... / I just hope...

〈스물다섯 스물하나〉 (2022)

**날씨가 너무 추운 겨울날, 친구가 '조금만 더 따뜻했으면 좋겠어.'라고 말했습니다.
이 말은 어떤 의미일까요?**

On a really cold winter day your friend tells you "조금만 더 따뜻했으면 좋겠어."
What could this mean?

ⓐ 원래 따뜻한 날씨가 좋다.

ⓑ 지금보다 날씨가 따뜻해지길 바란다.

ⓒ 지금처럼 추운 날씨가 계속되길 바란다.

-았/었- + -(으)면 + 좋- + -겠- + -어 = -았/었으면 좋겠어

-았/었으면 좋겠어 expresses a desire for a state or situation that is different from the present. Rather than describing an actual past event, it conveys hope or an imagination about something that did not happen or has not yet happened. For example, "날씨가 조금 더 따뜻했으면 좋겠어." means "I wish the weather were a little warmer," expressing a desire for warmer weather despite it being cold. It can also express regret or disappointment about past situations, like "그때 조금만 더 열심히 했으면 좋았을걸." (I wish I had tried a little harder back then.). This expression is used not only for simple wishes but also to reveal an imagination or regret about what might have been possible if the circumstances/situation had been different.

A 올 한 해 이루고 싶은 소망이 있어?
Do you have any new year's resolutions?

B 그냥 모두가 행복하고 ***건강했으면 좋겠어***. 작년은 너무 힘든 한 해였잖아.
I just hope everyone stays happy and healthy. Last year was so tough, wasn't it?

A 이 프로젝트가 언제 끝날까?
When will this project end?

B 빨리 ***끝났으면 좋겠어***. 너무 힘들어.
I just hope it will end soon. I'm exhausted.

A 어디서나 당찬 사람들을 보면 부러워. 나도 자신감이 ***넘쳤으면 좋겠어***.
I envy people who are bold wherever they go. I wish I could be brimming with confidence too.

B 대신 너는 배려심이 깊잖아. 나는 오히려 너의 그런 점이 부러운 걸?
But you're really considerate. Did you know, I envy that about you?

MP3 069

-(으)ㄹ 거야

I'll make sure... / I'm going to...

〈다 이루어질지니〉 (2025)

'나는 집에 갈 거야.'는 어떤 의미일까요?

What does "나는 집에 갈 거야." mean?

ⓐ 이미 집에 갔다.

ⓑ 집에 갈지 확실하지 않다.

ⓒ 집에 가는 것을 계획하고 있다.

-(으)ㄹ + 거(것) + (이) + -야 = -(으)ㄹ 거야

-(으)ㄹ 거야 is used to either express the speaker's future intention or decision, or to indicate a strong conjecture about something that has not yet happened. For example, when planning to go home after a dinner date with a friend, by saying "이제 집에 갈 거야." (I'm going home now.) reveals the speaker's plan and resolve to go home. Similarly, while watching a sports day competition, saying "아마 1반이 우승할 거야." (I'm going to bet that Class 1 will win.) conveys the speaker's strong belief that Class 1's will win, even though the actual result is unknown. This expression is informal and primarily used in everyday conversations.

Action!

A 부엌이 왜 이렇게 난장판이 됐어? 대체 뭘 하고 있는 거야?
Why is the kitchen in such a mess? What on earth are you doing?

B 〈오징어 게임〉에 나오는 달고나를 만들어 먹고 싶어서! 그냥 둬.
이따 다 만들고 나면 내가 ***치울 거야***.
I wanted to make and eat the dalgona candy from <Squid Game>!
Just leave me to it. I'm going to clean up after I'm done.

A 주말에 어디 ***갈 거야***?
Where are you going this weekend?

B 가족들과 바다에 ***갈 거야***.
I'm going to the beach with my family.

A 이번 주 축구 결승전 보러 갈까? 토트넘이랑 맨시티가 시합한대.
Want to go watch the soccer final this week? Tottenham and Manchester City are playing.

B 당연하지! 토트넘이 이번 경기에서 ***이길 거야***. 요즘 경기력 보면 맨시티는 상대가 안 돼.
Of course! I'm going to bet that Tottenham is going to win this game. Looking at their recent form, Manchester City is no match for them.

MP3 070

-았/었더라면

If I had...

〈폭싹 속았수다〉 (2025)

한 사람이 상을 받고 수상 소감을 말하고 있습니다. '만약 제가 그때 포기했더라면, 지금 이 자리에 없겠죠.' 이 말과 가장 의미가 가까운 문장은 무엇일까요?

A person is receiving an award and giving their acceptance speech. "만약 제가 그때 포기했더라면, 지금 이 자리에 없겠죠." Which sentence is closest in meaning to this statement?

ⓐ 그때 포기했으면 좋았을 텐데요.

ⓑ 그때 포기하지 않아서 다행이에요.

ⓒ 앞으로는 절대 포기하지 않을 거예요.

-았/었- + 더 + 라 + -(으)면 = -았/었더라면

-았/었더라면 is used when discussing hypothetical situations that did not occur in the past. It often conveys regret or an imagination of a different outcome. For example, "그때 공부했더라면 좋았을 텐데." (It would have been good if I had studied back then.) expresses regret over not studying in the past and the thought that studying would have led to a better result. This expression is typically followed by a sentence expressing wish or regret, like 좋았을 텐데.

Action!

A 내가 그때 그 사람에게 **사과했더라면** 상황이 달라졌을 거야.
If I had apologized to that person back then, the outcome would have been different.

B 맞아, 이제라도 늦지 않았으니 사과하는 게 어때?
Yeah, it's not too late even now. Why don't you apologize?

A 게임 그만 하고 얼른 저녁 먹어.
Stop playing games. Hurry up and eat dinner.

B 하던 것만 마저 하고 갈게요!
I'll just finish what I'm doing and then go!

A 저 열정으로 공부를 **했더라면** 서울대에 갔을 텐데.
If you had studied with that kind of passion, you would have gotten into Seoul National University.

A 오늘 왜 늦었어?
Why were you late today?

B 늦게 일어났어. 더 일찍 **일어났더라면** 제시간에 도착했을 텐데.
I woke up late. If I had gotten up earlier, I would have arrived on time.

MP3 071

-지 않을까?

Don't you think...? / Maybe it will...

〈미생〉 (2014)

'그 사람이 오지 않을까?'는 어떤 의미일까요?

What does "그 사람이 오지 않을까?" mean?

ⓐ 그 사람이 오지 않을 것이라고 확신한다.

ⓑ 그 사람이 이미 여기에 있다는 것을 알고 있다.

ⓒ 확실하지 않지만 그 사람이 올 수도 있다고 생각한다.

-지 + 않- + -(으)ㄹ까 = -지 않을까

-지 않을까? is used to speculate in a cautious way about the possibility of something happening or to seek agreement from the other person regarding one's own thoughts. For example, "그 사람이 오지 않을까?" (Don't you think that person will come?) expresses the speculation that there is a possibility that person will come. Therefore, it shares an opinion gently without stating his/her take definitively. While the affirmative form -(으)ㄹ까? directly asks about possibility or intention, -지 않을까? uses the negative form to imply a positive possibility while maintaining a polite, indirect tone.

Action!

A 내일은 드디어 10년 전에 묻은 타임캡슐을 열어 보기로 한 날이야!
Tomorrow is the day we're finally going to open the time capsule we buried 10 years ago!

B 벌써 시간이 그렇게 많이 지났다니…. 다른 친구들도 많이 올까?
I can't believe so much time has passed.... Do you think many of our other friends will come?

A 다 오지는 않더라도 몇 명은 ***오지 않을까***? 다들 어떻게 변했을지 궁금해!
Don't you think even if it isn't everyone, a few will show up? I wonder how everyone has changed!

A 지우한테 작은 화분을 선물로 주려고 하는데, 어떻게 생각해?
I'm thinking of giving Jiwoo a small plant as a gift. What do you think?

B 안 그래도 요즘 식물 키우는 데 푹 빠졌다고 하던데. ***좋아하지 않을까***?
I heard she's really into growing plants lately. Don't you think she'll like it?

A 다음 주 날씨가 어떨까?
What do you think the weather will be like next week?

B 영하니까 눈이 ***오지 않을까*** 싶어.
It's below freezing, so don't you think it will snow?

72

MP3 072

-고 나서

Then... / After...

〈선재 업고 튀어〉 (2024)

'밥 먹고 나서 영화를 보자.'는 무엇을 의미하나요?

What does "밥 먹고 나서 영화를 보자." mean?

ⓐ 밥 먹으면서 영화를 보자.

ⓑ 밥을 먹은 후에 영화를 보자.

ⓒ 먼저 영화를 보고, 그 후에 밥을 먹자.

-고 나다 + -아서 = -고 나서

-고 나서 is used to indicate that one action occurs after another action is completed. It is written by attaching -고 나서 to the verb stem, regardless of the stem ending in a consonant, and emphasizes the completion of the action in the first part of the sentence. For example, "밥 먹고 나서 영화를 보자." means "Let's watch a movie after we finish eating." While similar in meaning to "Let's watch a movie after eating," adding -고 나서 clearly identifies that the action listed in the first part of the sentence ended before the action in the second half of the sentence took place. It is primarily used to explain the sequence of events or to propose a plan.

A 내일 전주 여행 간다며? 계획은 세웠어?
You're going on a trip to Jeonju tomorrow, right? Have you made plans?

B 일단 한옥 마을을 ***구경하고 나서*** 비빔밥을 먹으러 갈 거야.
First, I'll check out the Hanok Village. Then, I'll go eat bibimbap.

A 어떤 스타일로 해 드릴까요?
What style would you like?

B 먼저 단발머리로 ***자르고 나서*** 갈색으로 염색을 하고 싶어요.
I want to get a bob cut first, then I'd like to dye it brown.

A 언제 이 영화 보러 갈까?
When should we go see this movie?

B 일 ***끝내고 나서*** 저녁에 보자.
Let's go watch it in the evening after I finish work.

73

MP3 073

-다가

While...

〈갯마을 차차차〉 (2021)

'집에 가다가 친구를 만났어.'는 어떤 의미일까요?

What does "집에 가다가 친구를 만났어." mean?

ⓐ 집에 가기 전에 친구를 만났다.

ⓑ 집에 가는 도중에 친구를 만났다.

ⓒ 집에 도착한 후에 친구를 만났다.

Meaning & Use~

-다가

-다가 is used to indicate a situation where another action or event suddenly interrupts an ongoing action. It is primarily used to describe unexpected situations and is attached directly to the verb stem. For example, "집에 가다가 친구를 만났어." (I ran into a friend while on my way home.) describes the situation of unexpectedly meeting a friend while heading home. It is also frequently used when narrating descriptions of events, particularly when an ongoing action stops and shifts to another situation, as in "공부하다가 잠이 들었어." (I fell asleep while studying.).

Action!

A 옷이 왜 그래요? 무슨 일 있었어요?
What happened to your clothes? Did something happen?

B 급하게 **오다가** 커피 들고 걸어오던 사람이랑 부딪혔어요.
I bumped into someone walking with a coffee while rushing over here.

A 왜 이렇게 늦었어? Why are you so late?

B 지하철 역으로 **가다가** 핸드폰을 놓고 온 걸 알게 돼서 다시 집에 갔다 왔어.
I realized I left my phone at home while on the way to the subway station, so I went back home.

A **운동하다가** 좀 쉬어도 되겠지?
Is it okay to take a break while exercising, right?

B 물론이지. 너무 무리하면 안 돼.
Of course. You shouldn't push yourself too hard.

MP3 074

-(으)ㄹ 만해

It's worth doing...

〈태풍상사〉 (2025)

다음 중 영화가 볼 가치가 있음을 나타내는 표현은?

Which of the following expressions indicates that the movie is worth watching?

ⓐ 이 영화는 볼 만해.

ⓑ 이 영화는 안 봐도 괜찮아.

ⓒ 이 영화를 보는 건 시간 낭비야.

-(으)ㄹ + 만하다 + -아 = -(으)ㄹ 만해

-(으)ㄹ 만해 is used to indicate that a particular action is worthwhile enough to do, justifiable, or feasible. For example, "이 영화는 볼 만해" means that the movie is worth watching, and "그는 차를 살 만한 형편이 못 된다." means the person who is being addressed is not in a financial position to buy a car. -ㄹ 만해 is used when the verb stem ends in a vowel and -을 만해 is used when it ends in a consonant. It is primarily used when recommending or evaluating an activity, experience, object, or place.

A 이 식당 어때?
How's this restaurant?

B 음식도 맛있고 분위기도 좋아서 ***가 볼 만해***.
The food is delicious and the atmosphere is nice, so it's worth checking out.

A 이 책 좀 두껍네. 읽기 힘들지 않아?
This book is pretty thick. Isn't it hard to read?

B 내용이 흥미로워서 끝까지 ***읽을 만해***.
He content is interesting, so it's worth reading until the end.

A 이 운동은 어려워 보여.
This exercise looks difficult.

B 하지만 효과가 좋아서 ***해 볼 만해***.
But it's effective, so it's worth trying.

MP3 075

75

-자마자

As soon as...

〈슬기로운 의사생활 1〉 (2020)

'집에 오자마자 잤어.'는 어떤 의미일까요?

What does "집에 오자마자 잤어." mean?

ⓐ 집에 오기 전에 이미 잠들었다.

ⓑ 집에 도착하자 곧바로 잠들었다.

ⓒ 집에 오고 나서 한참 뒤에 잠들었다.

-자마자

-자마자 indicates a situation where one action immediately follows the completion of another action. For example, "집에 가자마자 친구를 만났다." describes the moment when one arrived home, one met his/her friend. It is also used in contexts where an ongoing action abruptly comes to an end or shifts to another situation, such as "공부하다가 잠들었어." (I fell asleep as soon as I studied.). This expression is frequently used to highlight the rapid sequence of actions within the overall flow of a story.

Ⓐ 언제 전화할 거야?
When are you going to call me?

Ⓑ 회의 **끝나자마자** 전화할게.
I'll call you as soon as the meeting ends.

Ⓐ 와, 이 김치찌개 진짜 맛있다! 어떻게 만든 거야?
Wow, this kimchi stew is seriously delicious! How did you make it?

Ⓑ 어제 끓여 뒀어. 찌개는 **끓이자마자** 먹는 것보다 하루 지난 다음에 먹는 게 더 맛있더라고.
I cooked it yesterday. I find that stews taste better when consumed the day thereafter rather than as soon as its made.

Ⓐ 회사 면접 결과 나왔어?
Did the result of the company interview get released?

Ⓑ 아직 몰라. 결과 **나오자마자** 바로 알려 줄게.
I don't know (the result) yet. I'll let you know as soon as I find out.

76

MP3 076

-(으)ㄴ/는 편이야

Tend to be...

〈도깨비〉 (2016~2017)

다음 중 평소의 습관이나 경향을 나타내는 문장은 무엇인가요?

Which one of the following sentences indicates a habitual pattern or tendency?

ⓐ 어제는 비가 많이 왔어.

ⓑ 나는 지금 숙제를 하고 있어.

ⓒ 나는 야채를 자주 먹는 편이야.

-(으)ㄴ/는 + 편 + 이다 + -야 = -(으)ㄴ/는 편이야

-(으)ㄴ/는 편이야 expresses a certain tendency, inclination, or relatively consistent characteristic that the speaker possesses. Rather than exaggerating or making rigid assertions, it softens the statement by conveying the nuance that it is generally the case. -는 편이야 is used with action verbs in the present, -(으)ㄴ 편이야 for the past, and -(으)ㄴ 편이야 for adjectives or descriptions of a state. For example, "나는 야채를 자주 먹는 편이야." means "I tend to eat vegetables relatively often.", while "그 사람은 말이 적은 편이야." means "That person tends to be quiet."

A 매운 음식 잘 먹어요?

Do you handle spicy food well?

B 네, 잘 **먹는 편이에요**. 불닭 볶음면을 좋아해요.

Yeah, I tend to handle it pretty well. I like the buldak hot chicken flavor ramen.

A 보아하니 넌 집순이인 것 같아.

By the looks of it, I think you're a couch potato.

B 맞아, 집에서 쉬는 걸 **좋아하는 편이야**. 학교 가는 것 이외에는 주로 집에서 영화나 드라마를 보거나 가끔은 책을 읽어.

Yeah, I tend to enjoy relaxing at home. Besides going to school, I mostly stay home watching movies or dramas, or occasionally reading books.

A 강남대로가 빠르지 않아? 길도 넓고 차도 별로 없는데.

Isn't Gangnam-daero faster? The roads are wide and there aren't many cars.

B 그래도 테헤란로가 더 **빠른 편이야**. 신호등이 적어서 훨씬 빨리 갈 수 있어.

Still, Teheran-ro tends to be faster. There are fewer traffic lights, so you can get there quicker.

MP3 077

-(으)ㄴ/는 척하다

To pretend...

〈선재 업고 튀어〉 (2024)

'못 들은 척하다'는 무슨 의미일까요?

What does "못 들은 척하다" mean?

ⓐ 듣지 않고 대답하다

ⓑ 말을 못 들은 것처럼 행동하다

ⓒ 다른 사람의 말을 신경 쓰지 않다

-(으)ㄴ/는 + 척 + 하다 = -(으)ㄴ/는 척하다

-(으)ㄴ/는 척하다 is an expression that indicates pretending or acting as if something is true, even though it is not. -은 척하다 is used when the predicate stem ends in a consonant and -ㄴ 척하다 is used when ending in a vowel. In the case of action verbs, the past tense form -(으)ㄴ/는 is primarily used to convey the meaning of pretending to have done an action that did not actually occur. For example, "못 들은 척했어." (I pretended not to hear.) indicates that one actually heard but acted as if they hadn't.

콘서트장에서 At the concert venue

A 어? 너도 스트레이 키즈 좋아해? 여기서 만나다니 세상 정말 좁다!
Huh? You like Stray Kids too? What are the chances of bumping into you here! What a small world.

B 헉. 제발 우리 집엔 비밀로 해 줄래? 엄마 아빠한테 학원 ***가는 척하고*** 나왔단 말이야.
Gasp. Would you be able to keep this a secret from my family? I told my mom and dad that I was going to cram school, but pretended to do so.

A 걱정 안 ***하는 척하지만*** 사실 많이 걱정하고 있지?
You're pretending not to worry, but you're actually really concerned, right?

B 응, 맞아. 사실은 너무 불안해.
Yeah, you're right. I'm actually really anxious.

A 너 뭔가 숨기고 있지?
You're hiding something, aren't you?

B 아니야, 그런 거 없어. 그냥 좀 놀랐을 뿐이야.
No, there is nothing (I am hiding). I was just a little startled.

A ***아닌 척하지*** 마. 당황한 것 너무 티나. 솔직히 말해.
Don't pretend. You look caught by surprise. Tell me honestly.

MP3 078

78

-(으)ㄹ 리가 없어

There's no way...

〈도깨비〉 (2016~2017)

'그 사람이 내 말을 못 들었을 리가 없어.'는 어떤 의미일까요?

What does "그 사람이 내 말을 못 들었을 리가 없어." mean?

ⓐ 그 사람이 내 말을 들었다고 확신한다.

ⓑ 그 사람이 내 말을 듣는 것은 불가능하다고 확신한다.

ⓒ 그 사람이 내 말을 잘 듣지 못했을 것 같다고 추측한다.

-(으)ㄹ + 리 + 가 + 없어 = -(으)ㄹ 리가 없어

-(으)ㄹ 리가 없어 uses 리 as a dependent noun that emphasizes how there is absolutely no reason or basis for something. It is used when one is certain or skeptical that something is impossible or untrue. For example, "그 사람이 나를 좋아할 리가 없어." (There's no way that person likes me.) strongly denies the possibility that 'the person' likes the speaker. It is frequently used in conversations to express doubt or distrust about a situation.

Action!

A CCTV 확인은 다 끝났습니까?
Have you finished checking all the CCTV footage?

B 네. 그런데 목격자의 진술과 일치하는 인상착의를 가진 사람은 못 찾았습니다.
Yes. But we couldn't find anyone matching the description provided by the witness.

C ***그럴 리가 없어요***! 그날 그쪽 길로 가는 걸 분명히 봤다구요!
There is no way that can be the case! I told you, I clearly saw them heading that way that day!

A 비가 ***올 리가 없잖아***. 하늘이 너무 맑아.
There's no way it's going to rain. The sky is too clear.

B 요즘 날씨는 믿을 수 없어. 그러니까 우산 꼭 챙겨.
You can't trust the weather these days. So make sure to bring an umbrella.

A 그 사람 요즘 너한테 너무 친절한 거 아니야? 혹시 너를 좋아하는 거 아닐까?
Isn't that person being a little too nice to you lately? Could it be that he likes you?

B 나를 ***좋아할 리가 없어***. 그냥 예의로 잘해 주는 것뿐일 거야.
There's no way he likes me. He's simply just being polite.

79

MP3 079

-(으)ㄴ 적 있어?

Have you ever...

〈스물다섯 스물하나〉 (2022)

"한국에 가 본 적 있어?"는 무슨 뜻인가요?

What does "한국에 가 본 적 있어?" mean?

ⓐ 한국에 가 본 경험이 있는지 묻는 질문

ⓑ 한국에 가는 것에 대한 관심을 묻는 질문

ⓒ 한국에 가기로 한 계획이 있는지 묻는 질문

-(으)ㄴ + 적 + 있다/없다 = -(으)ㄴ 적 있다/없다

-(으)ㄴ 적 있다/없다 is an expression indicating whether one has experienced a certain event in the past. It is primarily used in the question form like …한 적 있어? to ask about someone's experience. In turn, when responding answers can be affirmative (…한 적 있다) or negative (…한 적 없다). Add -ㄴ after the verb stem when the predicate is an action verb and add -은 when it is a stative verb. This expression is also frequently used when sharing or comparing experiences.

Action!

A 한국 음식을 드셔 **본 적 있으세요**?
Have you ever tried Korean food?

B 네, 김치랑 불고기를 먹어 봤어요.
Yes, I've tried kimchi and bulgogi.

A 외국에서 **살았던 적 있으세요**?
Have you ever lived abroad?

B 네, 2년 동안 독일에서 살았어요.
Yes, I lived in Germany for two years.

A 마라톤 대회에 **참가한 적 있으세요**?
Have either of you ever taken part in a marathon?

B 네, 작년에 하프 마라톤에 참가했어요.
Yes, I participated in a half marathon last year.

C 아니요, 대회에는 **참가해 본 적 없어요**.
No. I've never participated in a competition.

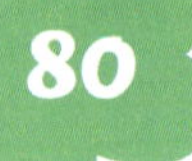

MP3 080

-(으)ㄴ/는 게 낫지 않아?

Isn't it better...?

〈으라차차 와이키키2〉 (2019)

다음 중 "그래도 해보는 게 낫지 않아?"를 사용할 수 없는 경우는?

Which one of the following situations is not appropriate for using "그래도 해보는 게 낫지 않아?"?

ⓐ 친구가 마지막 순간에 포기하려고 할 때

ⓑ 친구가 시험에 떨어져서 슬퍼하고 있을 때

ⓒ 친구가 이력서를 넣을지 말지 고민하고 있을 때

-(으)ㄴ/는 + -게 낫다 + -지 + 않다 + -아 = -는 게 낫지 않아?

-는 게 낫지 않아? is used to suggest a better action or choice, or to ask if an alternative is preferable. It is formed by adding -는 to the stem of an action verb and attaching it to -게 낫다. It's mainly used for friendly advice or suggestions, often preceded by 보다 when comparing two options or used with the adverb 차라리 (rather). In casual conversations, 보다는 is frequently shortened to 보단. For example, "늦게 가는 것보단 지금 가는 게 낫지 않아?" (Isn't it better to go now than to wait?) indicates the speaker believes going now is best.

A 기타를 배워 보고 싶어서 학교 동아리에 가입했어.
I joined the school club because I wanted to try learning how to play the guitar.

B 처음 악기를 배울 때는 동아리보단 학원에 ***등록하는 게 낫지 않아***?
When you're first learning an instrument, isn't it better to enroll in a music academy instead of a club?

A 새 휴대폰 살까? 지금 사용 중인 폰이 배터리가 빨리 닳아서 불편해.
Should I buy a new phone? It's annoying because my current phone's battery drains out so fast.

B 지금 사는 것보다 조금 더 ***기다리는 게 낫지 않아***? 곧 세일할 텐데 그때 사면 더 저렴할 거야.
Shouldn't you wait a bit longer instead of buying a new phone? There'll soon be a sale. You should buy one then when it is cheaper.

A 내일 출발해도 괜찮을까? 갑자기 일이 생길 수도 있을 것 같아서 고민 중이야.
Is it okay to leave tomorrow? I'm worried something might come up suddenly.

B 차라리 오늘 ***가는 게 낫지 않아***? 오늘 가면 시간도 더 많고 미리 준비할 수 있어.
Wouldn't it be better to go today? If you go today, you'll have more time and you'll be able to prepare in advance.

MP3 081

81

-기도 하고…

Also… / Both… and…

〈멜로가 체질〉 (2019)

"그 영화는 재미있기도 하고 감동적이기도 했어."는 어떤 의미일까요?

What does "그 영화는 재미있기도 하고 감동적이기도 했어." mean?

ⓐ 그 영화는 재미있고 감동적이었어.

ⓑ 그 영화는 재미있지만 감동적이지 않았어.

ⓒ 그 영화는 감동적이지만 재미있지 않았어.

-기 + 도 + 하다 + -고 = -기도 하고

-기도 하고 is used to list two or more qualities, actions, or characteristics about a single object or situation. Within the same sentence, it can express positive qualities, negative qualities, or different qualities together. It is formed by adding -기도 하다 to the stem of a verb or adjective, and is often used repeatedly to create a sense of parallelism. For example, "그 영화는 재밌기도 하고 슬프기도 해." means that the movie conveys both fun and sadness simultaneously. This expression is frequently used to describe emotions, personality traits, states, or actions together.

A 새로 온 직원은 어때?

How's the new employee?

B ***친절하기도 하고 똑똑하기도 해서*** 같이 있으면 기분이 좋아.

He's kind and he's also smart, so it's nice to be around him.

A 회사 구내식당 리모델링 끝났다고 하던데, 혹시 가 보셨어요?

I heard the remodeling of the company cafeteria is complete. Have you been yet?

B 네, 어제 가 보니까 예전보다 ***넓어지기도 하고***, 음식 맛도 훨씬 좋아진 것 같더라고요.

Yeah, I went yesterday. It's bigger than before, and the food seems also way tastier compared to before.

A 여행은 어땠어? 지친 일상에서 벗어나서 정말 좋았을 것 같은데.

How was your trip? It must have been great to escape the exhausting routine.

B ***즐겁기도 하고 힘들기도 했지만***, 새로운 경험이 많아서 기억에 남을 것 같아.

It was fun and it was also tiring. But I had so many new experiences that it'll be memorable.

MP3 082

-(으)ㄹ 수밖에 없어

Can't help... / It's inevitable ...

〈은중과 상연〉 (2025)

다음 중 다른 방법이 없음을 표현한 문장은 무엇인가요?

Which one of the following sentences expresses that there is no alternative?

ⓐ 그말이야.

ⓑ 그 말을 믿지 않을 거야.

ⓒ 그 말을 믿을 수밖에 없어.

-(으)ㄹ + 수밖에 + 없다 = -(으)ㄹ 수밖에 없다

-(으)ㄹ 수밖에 없어 expresses an unavoidable situation which consequently leads to making something inevitable to do. It is used by attaching the structure -(으)ㄹ 수밖에 없다 to the verb stem, emphasizing an unavoidable or inevitable situation. For example, "그 말을 믿을 수밖에 없어." (I can't help but believe that.) means there is no alternative but to trust those words. This expression is often used when the speaker feels powerless to change the situation or senses it is inescapable, inevitable.

A 왜 그 계획에 동의했어?
Why did you agree to that plan?

B 다른 방법이 없어서 **따를 수밖에 없었어**.
I couldn't help but go along with it as there were no other means.

A 왜 이렇게 긴장했어? 그냥 가족들이랑 가볍게 식사 한 끼 하는 것 뿐인데.
Why are you so nervous? It's just a casual meal with my family.

B 그래도 너희 가족을 처음 뵙는 자리잖아. 긴장이 **될 수밖에 없지**!
But it's my first time meeting your family! I can't help but be nervous!

A 이번 프로젝트 왜 이렇게 열심히 준비해?
Why are you working so hard on this project?

B 마감일이 다가와서 열심히 **일할 수밖에 없어**. 팀원들도 다들 바빠.
The deadline is approaching, so I can't help but work hard. Everyone on the team is busy too.

MP3 083

83

-(으)ㄹ 필요가 없어

No need to...

〈슬기로운 의사생활 1〉 (2020)

'점심을 많이 먹었으니까 저녁을 먹을 필요가 없어'는 어떤 의미일까요?

What does "점심을 많이 먹었으니까 저녁을 먹을 필요가 없어" mean?

ⓐ 세 끼를 꼭 챙겨 먹는 것은 중요하다.

ⓑ 점심에 과식했으니 저녁을 굶어도 된다.

ⓒ 점심을 먹었으니 저녁을 꼭 먹어야 한다.

-(으)ㄹ + 필요 + 가 + 없다 + -어 = -(으)ㄹ 필요가 없어

-(으)ㄹ 필요가 없어 indicates that a certain action/state is unnecessary or not requested. It is formed by adding -ㄹ to verb stems ending in a vowel and -을 to those ending in a consonant, followed by the phrase 필요가 없다 (there is no need). It can also be combined with adjectives. For example, a sentence like "그렇게 심각할 필요가 없어." (There's no need to be that serious.) expresses how it's not necessary to get a serious degree and "걱정할 필요가 없어." (There's no need to worry.) reassures someone that the act of worrying is entirely unnecessary. This expression is frequently used to alleviate negative feelings, offer advice, persuade, or reduce unnecessary actions.

A 이번 앨범이 인기가 없을까 봐 걱정 돼. 혹시 망하면 어쩌지?
I'm concerned about this album review. What if it flops?

B 아니야, 너의 스타일이 분명히 통할 거야. ***걱정할 필요가 없어***.
No, your style will definitely resonate with others. No need to worry.

A 이 문서 다시 한 번 점검해야 할까? 내용이 중요해서 실수하면 안 되거든.
Should I examine this document one more time? The content is important, so I can't afford any mistakes.

B 아니, ***점검할 필요가 없어***. 내가 이미 한 번 더 검토했거든.
No, there is no need to examine it again. I've already reviewed it again.

A 오늘 밤 외식할까? 매일 똑같은 것만 먹어서 지겹지?
Should we eat out tonight? Aren't you tired of eating the same thing every day?

B 아니, 꼭 ***그럴 필요는 없어***. 너랑 같이 있으면 매일 같은 것만 먹어도 좋은 걸.
No, there is no need to do so by all means. When I'm with you, even eating the same thing every day is fine.

MP3 084

-거든(요)

Actually...

〈스물다섯 스물하나〉 (2022)

'어제 친구와 싸웠어요. 저한테 거짓말을 했던 걸 알게 됐거든요.'의 의미로 적절한 것은?

Which of the following has the same meaning of "어제 친구와 싸웠어요. 저한테 거짓말을 했던 걸 알게 됐거든요."?

ⓐ 친구랑 싸우는 도중에 친구가 거짓말을 했다.

ⓑ 친구는 우리가 싸운 이유에 대해 거짓말을 했다.

ⓒ 친구랑 싸운 이유는 친구가 거짓말을 했기 때문이다.

-거든(요)

-거든(요) is used to explain a reason or provide additional context. It can be used to explain reasons or provide background knowledge to the listener, convey nuances of admiration or pride, or serve as a prelude to an upcoming conversation. Attaching -거든 or -거든요 to the stem of a verb or adjective conveys a variety of feelings. Depending on the tone, it can range from a strong emphasis to a friendly or gentle explanation.

A 퇴근 안 하세요?

You aren't going to call it a day?

B 아, 내일이 프로젝트 ***마감일이거든요***. 아침까지 끝내야 해서 아마 오늘 회사에서 밤새워야 할 것 같아요.

Oh, tomorrow is actually the project deadline. I have to finish it by the morning, so I'm most likely going to pull an all-nighter at the office.

A 어제는 늦게까지 같이 있었잖아. 오늘은 왜 이렇게 일찍 가야 해?

Yesterday, we stayed up until late together. Why do you have to leave so early today?

B *(한숨)* 내일 아침에 중요한 회의가 있어서 오늘 집에서 준비해야 ***되거든***.

(Sighs) I have an important meeting tomorrow, so I actually have to prepare things at home today.

A 그 사람을 왜 좋아해?

Why do you like him?

B 누구에게나 친절한 ***사람이거든***. 지난번에 다친 고양이를 치료해 주는 모습을 봤는데, 그때 정말 마음이 따뜻한 사람이라는 걸 알게 됐어.

He's actually kind to everyone. The other day, I saw him treating an injured cat. That's when I realized he's a really warm-hearted guy.

85

MP3 085

-아/어도 돼?

Is it okay/fine...?

〈미생〉 (2014)

다음 중 "여기 앉아도 돼요?"를 사용할 수 없는 경우는?

Which one of the following situations is not appropriate for using "여기 앉아도 돼요?"?

ⓐ 카페에서 빈자리가 있어 상대에게 물을 때

ⓑ 도서관에서 빈자리가 있어서 앉아도 되는지 옆 사람에게 물을 때

ⓒ 지하철에서 앉아 있으면서 서 있는 사람에게 자리를 양보하려고 할 때

-아/어도 + 되다 = -아/어도 돼?

-아/어도 되다 is an expression used when asking or stating whether a certain action is permitted, or whether it's okay for the other person to act that way. While it fundamentally indicates permission or acceptance, in actual conversations it's frequently used not only for simple permission requests but also to confirm the appropriateness or validity of an action, or to raise concerns about it. For example, "이렇게 해도 돼?" (Is it okay to do it in this way?) could mean asking for permission, but depending on the context, it could also confirm the legitimacy of a method or action, like "이 방식이 맞아?" (Is this approach correct?) or "그렇게 해도 문제가 없겠어?" (Would doing it in that way be problematic?). It is also used when one criticizes or opposes someone else's actions as morally or socially inappropriate, as in "저런 걸 시켜도 돼?" (Is it okay to make them do that?). It can be conveyed with various levels of politeness: informal -아/어도 돼?, polite -아/어도 돼요?, and formal -아/어도 됩니까?. Similar expressions include -아/어도 괜찮다 (it's okay to do that), -아/어도 좋아요 (it's fine to do that), and -아/어도 무방합니다 (it's acceptable to do that). The opposite meaning is expressed with -(으)면 안 되다 (you must not do that), indicating disapproval or prohibition. It's used not only for simple permission-based requests but also to confirm the appropriateness of a method, as in "이렇게 해도 돼?" (Is it fine if I do it this way?).

A 오늘 너무 덥네, 창문 **열어도 돼**?
It's so hot today, is it okay if I open the window?

B 물론이지! 조금 환기시키는 게 좋겠어.
Of course! It'd be good to get some fresh air.

A 오늘 저녁에 데이트하기로 했는데, 이 옷 **입어도 돼**?
I have a date tonight, is it fine if I wear this outfit?

B 정말? 당연히 입어도 되지! 더 필요한 건 없어?
Really? It's your first date? Of course you can wear it! Do you need anything else?

A 미안한데, 잠깐 전화 좀 하고 **와도 돼**? 급한 일이 생겼어.
Sorry, is it okay if I step out for a quick call? Something urgent came up.

B 응, 괜찮아. 빨리 끝내고 와.
Yeah, sure. Finish up quickly and come back.

86

MP3 086

-기 싫어

To not want to...

〈은중과 상연〉 (2025)

다음 중 '아침에 일찍 일어나기 싫어요.' 라는 문장 후에 오면 가장 자연스러운 말은?

Which one of the following would be the most natural thing to say after the sentence "아침에 일찍 일어나기 싫어요."?

ⓐ 그래서 항상 늦게까지 잠을 자요.

ⓑ 그래서 일찍 일어나서 운동을 시작했어요.

ⓒ 그래서 친구와 늦게 저녁을 먹으러 갔어요.

-기 + 싫- + -어 = -기 싫어

-기 싫어 expresses unwillingness or reluctance to perform an action. It is formed by adding -기 to the verb stem, followed by 싫다. The informal form is -기 싫어 and the polite form is -기 싫어요. For example, "일하기 싫어." (I don't want to work.) means one does not have a desire to work. It is frequently used in casual conversations to directly express feelings or intentions, and can be used in a playful or serious tone depending on the situation. Whereas -기 싫다 often conveys feelings more directly and strongly, a similar expression, -고 싶지 않다 expresses refusal in a somewhat neutral and indirect manner.

A 요즘 운동이 부족하다고 하지 않았어? 같이 운동하러 갈래?
Didn't you say that you haven't been exercising enough lately? Wanna go work out together?

B 맞아, 근데 지금은 ***운동하기 싫어***. 너무 피곤하고 그냥 누워 있고 싶어.
Yeah, but I don't want to work out right now. I'm too tired and just want to lie down.

A 음, 그래도 조금만 움직이면 기분이 좋아질지도 몰라. 가벼운 산책이라도 할까?
Hmm, but maybe moving around a little could make you feel better. How about a light walk?

A 오늘 생일 파티 간다며? 준비 안 해?
You're going to a birthday party today, right? Don't you have to prepare (to go)?.

B 아···. 솔직히 오늘은 ***나가기 싫다***. 사람들 만나기엔 좀 지치네.
Ah.... Honestly, I don't want to go out today. I'm a bit too drained to see people.

A 이번 영화에서 정말 신들린 연기력을 보여 주셔서 많은 호평을 받으셨잖아요.
You know, you really showed some divine acting skills in this movie and received a lot of praise.

B 하하, 감사합니다. 어렵게 얻은 기회인데, 못한다는 얘기 ***듣기 싫어서*** 정말 열심히 했어요.
Haha, thank you. It was a hard-earned opportunity, and I really didn't want to hear negative criticism, so I worked really hard.

87

-았/었어야 했는데

Should have...

〈나빌레라〉 (2021)

다음 중 '-았/었어야 했는데'의 뜻을 가장 잘 설명한 것은 무엇입니까?

Which one of the following best explains the meaning of "-았/었어야 했는데"?

ⓐ 미래에 해야 할 일을 계획하는 상황

ⓑ 하고 싶지 않은 일을 억지로 하는 상황

ⓒ 해야 할 일을 하지 않아서 후회하는 상황

-았/었- + -어야 하다 + -았/었- + -는데 = -았/었어야 했는데

-았/었어야 했는데 expresses regret or disappointment over something that should have been done but wasn't. It is formed by adding the past tense ending -았/었- to the verb stem, is combined with -아/어야 하다 to indicate obligation, and then -(으)ㄴ는데 is added to explain the situation as background context or to connect to the content that follows. For example, "일찍 출발했어야 했는데." (I should have left earlier.) expresses regret and reflection over not having departed sooner. This expression is primarily used when looking back on past actions or choices to acknowledge mistakes or convey disappointment.

Action!

A 생일 파티 재밌었어? 많이들 왔어?
Did you have fun at the birthday party? Did a lot of people come?

B 초대 받아서 **참석했어야 했는데** 못 갔어. 선약이 있었어.
I should've gone since I was invited, but I couldn't make it. I had another plan.

A 부모님께 전화 드렸어? 오랜만에 통화한다고 하지 않았어?
Did you call your parents? Didn't you say it'd been a long time since you last spoke on the phone?

B 어머나, 전화 **드렸어야 했는데** 일이 많아서 까먹어 버렸어.
Oh my, I should've called them. I had so much going on, I completely forgot.

A 그럼 지금이라도 전화 드려. 기다리고 계실 거야.
Then call them now. They'll be waiting.

A 어제 데이트 허둥대며 가더니 약속 시간에 늦지 않았지?
You were rushing off to your date yesterday. You weren't late for your appointment, were you?

B 아, 늦었어. 더 일찍 **출발했어야 했는데** 길이 너무 막혔어.
Oh, I was late. I should've left earlier, but the traffic was terrible.

A 에휴, 다음엔 시간을 넉넉히 잡아야겠다. 상대방이 좀 서운했겠네.
Ugh, Next time, you should make sure to allow for plenty of time. Your date must've been disappointed.

88

MP3 088

-더니

As a result...

〈그 해 우리는〉 (2021)

다음 중 '배탈이 났구나' 앞에 오기에 자연스러운 표현은?

Which one of the following expressions would naturally follow "배탈이 났구나"?

ⓐ 많이 먹더니

ⓑ 병원에 가더니

ⓒ 자전거를 타더니

-더니

-더니 is used to describe a result or a change observed after a specific action or state, and is attached to the verb stem. For example, "많이 먹었더니 배가 아프다." (I ate a lot and, as as result, I have a stomach ache.) connects the action of eating a lot with the result of stomach pain. When describing the speaker's own experience and its outcome, the past tense ending -았/었- is added. When describing someone else's situation, it is used in the present tense without the past tense ending -았/었-. For instance, whereas "잘하려고 노력했더니 좋은 결과를 얻었네." (I tried hard and, as a result, got good results.) evaluates one's own actions and the respective outcome, "잘하려고 노력하더니 좋은 결과를 얻었네." (He tried hard and, as a result, got good results.) evaluates someone else's actions and their outcome.

A 어제 밤새웠어?
Did you stay up all night?

B 응, **밤새웠더니** 오늘 너무 피곤해. 게다가 오늘은 평소보다 일이 많아서 잠깐 쉴 시간도 없네.
Yeah, I'm really tired today as a result of staying up all night. Plus, I have more work than usual today, so I don't even have a moment to rest.

A 왜 기분이 안 좋아 보여? 무슨 일 있었어?
Why do you look so down? Did something happen?

B 너무 오래 **걸었더니** 다리가 아파. 그래서 기분도 좀 가라앉았고.
My legs hurt as a result of walking for a long time. That's why I'm feeling a bit down too.

A 선희가 매일 아침 조깅을 **하더니** 체력이 정말 좋아졌어.
Sunhee's stamina has really improved as a result of jogging every morning.

B 맞아, 요즘 얼굴도 더 건강해 보이더라.
Yeah, her face looks healthier these days too.

89

MP3 089

-(으)ㄴ/는가 보다, -나 보다

Looks like... / I guess...

〈조립식 가족〉 (2024)

'다들 지쳐서 조용한가 보다.'라고 말할 수 있는 상황은?

In which situation would you say, "다들 지쳐서 조용한가 보다."?

ⓐ 아무도 말을 하지 않는다.

ⓑ 사람들이 즐겁게 놀고 있다.

ⓒ 주변이 너무 시끄러워서 대화하기가 힘들다.

-(으)ㄴ/는가, -나 + 보다 = -(으)ㄴ/는가 보다, -나 보다

-(으)ㄴ/는가 보다, -나 보다 is an expression that is used when making an inference based on an observation or circumstance. It is attached to adjectives as -(으)ㄴ/는가 보다 and to verbs as -나 보다. For example, "저 사람은 바쁜가 보다." (That person looks like he is busy.) infers that a person is busy based on their actions or expressions. It is primarily used in everyday conversations and thoughts are conveyed in a non-definite, gentle tone. -(으)ㄴ/는가 봐, -나 봐 is frequently used in casual conversations.

A 사무실이 왜 이렇게 조용해? 사람들이 다 어디 간 거야?
Why is the office so quiet? Where did everyone go?

B 다들 **퇴근했나 봐**. 벌써 7시야.
It looks like everyone's already left. It's 7 o'clock already.

A 나도 가야겠다. 이렇게 늦었는지 몰랐네.
I should call it a day too. Didn't realize it was this late.

A 민재가 왜 연락이 없는지 알아? 카톡에 답장도 없고 이메일도 안 읽는 것 같은데.
Do you know why Minjae isn't responding? He's not replying to KakaoTalk or reading emails.

B 요즘 **바쁜가 보다**. 일이 많아서 연락할 시간이 **없나 봐**.
It looks like he's quite busy lately. He's probably swamped with work and it looks like he doesn't have time to reach out.

A 흠, 그래? 항상 연락을 잘했었는데. 다른 일이 있는지 좀 걱정되네.
Hmm, really? He was always good about keeping in touch. I'm a bit worried something else might be going on.

A 밖이 갑자기 시끄러운데 무슨 일 있는 거야?
It suddenly got noisy outside. What's going on?

B 축제 **준비하나 봐**. 아까 보니까 사람들이 무대 세우고 있더라.
It looks like they're preparing for a festival. I saw people setting up a stage earlier.

MP3 090

-(으)ㄹ까 봐

To be worried/afraid...

〈폭싹 속았수다〉 (2025)

'늦을까 봐 서둘렀어.'는 어떤 의미일까요?

What does "늦을까 봐 서둘렀어." mean?

ⓐ 늦을지 몰라 서둘렀어.

ⓑ 일부러 늦으려고 했어.

ⓒ 늦지 않아서 여유를 부렸어.

-(으)ㄹ까 + 보다 + -아 = -(으)ㄹ까 봐

-(으)ㄹ까 봐 expesses worry or fear about the possibility of something happening. For example, "늦을까 봐 서둘렀어." means "I hurried because I was worried I might be late." -을까 봐 is used when the verb stem ends in a consonant and -ㄹ까 봐 is used when it ends in a vowel. It can also combine with adjectives to express concern about a state, like "추울까 봐 옷을 더 껴입었어." (I wore more layers because I was worried it might be cold.). It is primarily used when explaining why certain actions were taken to prepare for or prevent negative outcomes. The speaker's psychological state is revealed when phrases like 걱정돼 (I'm worried) or 두려워 (I'm afraid) follow -(으)ㄹ까 봐.

Action!

A 와…. 음식 준비 너무 많이 한 것 아니야?
Wow.... Isn't this way too much food?

B 손님들이 많이 ***올까 봐*** 넉넉하게 준비했어.
I was worried that a lot of guests would come so I prepared a lot.

A 내가 추천한 그 영화 봤어?
Did you watch that movie I recommended?

B 아니. 러닝 타임이 너무 길더라구. 그래서 ***지루해질까 봐*** 다른 영화를 봤어. 다음에 혼자 있을 때 볼게!
No. The length of the movie was too long. I was worried I'd get bored, so I watched a different movie. I'll watch it next time when I'm alone!

A 어디 아파? 왜 약을 먹었어?
Where does it hurt? Why did you take medicine?

B 머리가 ***아플까 봐*** 걱정돼서 미리 먹었어.
I took in advance as I was worried my head might hurt.

A 정말? 미리 약을 먹는다는 이야기는 처음 듣는다.
Really? This is the first time I've heard of taking medicine preventively.

MP3 091

-기로 했어

Decided to...

〈미생〉 (2014)

다음 중 '내일부터 한국어 공부를 더 열심히 하기로 했어.'와 다른 의미를 가진 문장은 무엇인가요?

Which one of the following has a different meaning from "내일부터 한국어 공부를 더 열심히 하기로 했어."?

ⓐ 내일부터 한국어 공부를 더 열심히 할 거야.

ⓑ 내일부터 한국어 공부를 더 열심히 하려고 해.

ⓒ 내일부터 한국어 공부를 더 열심히 하면 안 되지.

-기 + (으)로 + 하다 = -기로 하다

-기로 하다 indicates a decision to take a certain action or make a plan. It is formed by attaching -기로 to the verb stem and combining it with 하다. In informal speech, it is written as -기로 했어, and in polite speech it is written as -기로 했어요. For example, "친구랑 영화를 보기로 했어." (I decided to watch a movie with my friend.) expresses the decision to watch a movie. This expression is primarily used to emphasize a decision made after careful consideration or discussion, and it is also used to convey future plans or indicate a promise.

Action!

A 주말에 뭐 하실 거예요?
What are you doing this weekend?

B 가족이랑 캠핑을 ***가기로 했어요***.
I decided to go camping with my family.

A 우리 오빠가 다음 달에 ***결혼하기로 했어***.
My brother has decided to get married next month.

B 지금 사귀고 있는 그 여자분이랑? 잘 됐네. 축하한다고 전해 줘.
With that lady he is seeing now? That's great. Congratulate him on my behalf.

A 오늘은 집중해서 ***공부하기로 했어***. 어제는 좀 쉬었거든.
I decided to focus on studying today. I rested a bit yesterday.

B 공부할 때, 어디에서 하는 게 제일 집중이 잘 돼?
When you study, where do you find it best to concentrate?

A 도서관이나 카페. 어려운 공부는 도서관에서, 외우는 공부는 카페에서 하는 게 집중이 잘 돼.
The library or a cafe. I find it easier to study difficult material in the library and concentrate well on memorization at a cafe.

92

MP3 092

-는 바람에

Due to... (negative consequence)

〈미생〉 (2014)

다음 중 '-는 바람에'를 잘못 쓴 표현은?

Which one of the following incorrectly uses "-는 바람에"?

ⓐ 가격이 싼 바람에 핸드폰이 잘 팔린다.

ⓑ 강풍이 부는 바람에 비행기가 취소됐다.

ⓒ 긴장한 바람에 말하기 시험에서 떨어졌다.

-는 + 바람에 = -는 바람에

-는 바람에 is used to explain the reason for an unexpected, usually negative outcome. For example, "비가 오는 바람에 소풍이 취소되었어." indicates that the picnic was canceled due to the rain. This expression cannot be used with adjectives; instead, it is attached to a verb stem. It is primarily used to emphasize situations that led to an undesired result. Furthermore, it is only used in positive situations when an unexpected result occurs. Since this expression explains the reason for an event that has already happened, the past tense always follows -는 바람에. Therefore, it cannot be used with imperatives or sentences that are requests.

A 컴퓨터가 ***고장나는 바람에*** 일을 못 했어요.
I couldn't get any work done due to my computer breaking down.

B 정말 불편했겠네요. 중요한 자료는 다 저장해 놓았어요?
That must have been really inconvenient. Were you able to save all your important files?

A 알람 시계가 안 ***울리는 바람에*** 지각했어.
I was late due to my alarm clock not going off.

B 벌써 몇 번째냐?
How many times has this happened now?

A 오늘 비가 많이 ***오는 바람에*** 소풍을 못 갈 줄 알았는데, 날씨가 금방 개었어요.
I thought we wouldn't be able to go on the picnic due to the heavy rainfall today, but the weather quickly cleared up.

B 예정대로 소풍 갈 수 있어서 다행이에요. 아니면 아이들이 많이 실망했을 거예요.
It's a relief we could go on the picnic as planned. Otherwise, the children would have been really disappointed.

MP3 093

93 (-(으)ㄴ/는) 덕분에

Thanks to...

〈도깨비〉 (2016~2017)

다음 중 '(-(으)ㄴ/는) 덕분에'가 올바르게 쓰이지 않은 문장은?

Which one of the following sentences uses "(-(으)ㄴ/는) 덕분에" incorrectly?

ⓐ 가르쳐 주신 덕분에 이번 시험을 잘 봤어요.

ⓑ 시간을 잘못 안 덕분에 그 사람을 못 만났어요.

ⓒ 알려 주신 덕분에 좋은 기회를 얻을 수 있었어요.

(-(으)ㄴ) + 덕분 + 에 = (-(으)ㄴ) 덕분에

(-(으)ㄴ) 덕분에 indicates that a positive outcome or situation occurred due to someone's help or influence, and is used to express gratitude or appreciation. 덕분에 used after nouns, -은 덕분에 used after nouns or verb stems ending in consonants, and -ㄴ 덕분에 after verb stems ending in vowels. For example, "네 덕분에 시험을 잘 봤어." (I did well on the exam thanks to you.) means that the speaker achieved a good result on the exam due to the other person's help. Similar expressions include -기 때문에 (because of), which explains the cause in a neutral way, and (으)로 인해 used in formal or polite sentences. In contrast, -(으)ㄴ 덕분에 emphasizes a positive outcome and conveys gratitude.

Action!

A 지난번에 얘기한 행사는 잘 끝났어요?
Did the event we talked about last time go well?

B 네, ***도와주신 덕분에*** 무사히 잘 끝낼 수 있었어요.
Yes, we managed to wrap it up well thanks to your help.

A 업무가 너무 많은데 ***챗GPT 덕분에*** 겨우 해내고 있어요.
We have a lot of work tasks to address, but thanks to Chat GPT we barely finished everything.

B 저도 번역 업무나 리서치 업무에 덕을 많이 보고 있어요. 없을 때는 어떻게 살았나 몰라요.
I am also making good use of Chat GPT for translation and research work tasks. I don't know how I lived without it.

A ***네 덕분에*** 운동을 시작했어. 운동을 하니 몸도 마음도 건강해진 것 같아.
I started exercising thanks to you. Working out seems to have made both my body and mind healthier.

B 그렇게 말해 주니 고맙네. 언제 한 번 체육관에 같이 가자.
I appreciate you saying that. Let's hit the gym together sometime.

94

MP3 094

-(으)면 할수록

The more ..., the more...

〈사내맞선〉 (2022)

'한국어 공부를 하면 할수록' 다음에 나올 수 없는 문장은?

Which one would not follow the sentence "한국어 공부를 하면 할수록"?

ⓐ 망친다.

ⓑ 더 잘하게 된다.

ⓒ 더 어렵게 느껴진다.

-(으)면 + 하- + -ㄹ수록 = -(으)면 할수록

-(으)면 할수록 expresses when one thing increases or repeats, another related thing also increases or changes respectively. When the verb stem ends in a consonant, use -으면 할수록; when it ends in a vowel, use -면 할수록. For example, "공부하면 할수록 실력이 늘어." means that the more you study, the more your skills improve. This expression is used to describe how the more an action or condition is done, the resulting outcome or state changes gradually as a result.

Action!

A 영화를 ***보면 볼수록*** 다양한 감정을 느낄 수 있어서 좋아요.
I love how the more I watch movies, the more diverse emotions I feel.

B 책을 읽어도 마찬가지지 않아요?
Isn't it the same when you read books?

A 물론 그렇지만 영화는 시각적인 매체라 감정 전달이 더 즉각적인 거 같아요.
Of course, but movies are a visual medium, so the emotional impact feels more immediate.

A 영주는 ***만나면 만날수록*** 더 매력적인 친구야.
The more you meet Yeongju, the more charming she comes across.

B 맞아. 취미도 많고 하고 싶은 것도 많은 친구라, 같이 있으면 시간 가는 줄 모르겠어.
That's right. She has so many hobbies and things she wants to do, so when we're together, I lose MP3 of the time.

A 골프 치러 자주 다니는 것 같은데, 실력이 많이 늘었겠네요.
I heard you go golfing often. Your skills must have improved a lot.

B 이상하게 골프는 ***치면 칠수록*** 어려워지는 것 같아요.
Strangely, the more I play golf, the harder it seems to get.

MP3 095

-고 싶어(요)

Want to...

〈이상한 변호사 우영우〉 (2022)

다음 중 '나는 지금 쉬고 싶어'와 같은 의미를 가진 문장은 무엇인가요?

Which one of the following sentences has the same meaning as "나는 지금 쉬고 싶어"?

ⓐ 나는 쉬어야만 해.

ⓑ 나는 지금 쉬는 중이야.

ⓒ 나는 지금 쉬었으면 좋겠어.

-고 + 싶- + -어(요) = -고 싶어(요)

-고 싶어요 indicates a desire or wish for a certain action or state, most commonly used to express hope or aspiration. It is formed by adding -고 싶다 to the verb stem. -고 싶어 is used in casual contexts and -고 싶어요 in formal contexts. For example, "나는 여행을 가고 싶어." expresses the desire to go on a trip. Depending on the context, 싶다 can convey not only a simple desire but also: a regret "다시 가고 싶다." (I want to go again.), nostalgia "그때로 돌아가고 싶다." (I want to go back to that time.), or an indirect suggestion "같이 가고 싶으시면 말씀하세요." (Let me know if you want to go together.).

Action!

A 여행을 **가고 싶어**.

I want to go on a trip.

B 나도 제주도 가 **보고 싶은데** 우리 이번 주말에 제주도로 떠나 볼까?

I've been wanting to visit Jeju Island too. How about we head to Jeju this weekend?

A 택시 **타고 싶지만** 돈이 없으니까 지하철을 타야겠지?

I want to take a taxi, but since we don't have much money, we'll have to take the subway, right?

B 돈도 돈이지만 택시타면 길이 막혀서 지각할 수 있어.

Money aside, if we take a taxi, we might get stuck in traffic and be late.

A 무슨 책을 **읽고 싶어요**?

What kind of book do you want to read?

B 장르 불문하고 한국어로 된 책을 **읽어 보고 싶어요**.

I want to read a book written in Korean, regardless of the genre.

MP3 096

이/가 아니라

It's not... but...

〈사내맞선〉 (2022)

'선영이는 의사가 아니라 선생님이야'라고 말했을 때, 선영이의 직업은?

When someone says "선영이는 의사가 아니라 선생님이야" what is Sunyoung's profession?

ⓐ 의사

ⓑ 선생님

ⓒ 의사인 동시에 선생님

이/가 아니- + -라 = 이/가 아니라

이/가 아니라 is an expression indicating that something is not one thing (the preceding content) but another (the following content). Use 이 아니라 after nouns ending in a consonant, and 가 아니라 after nouns ending in a vowel. For example, "나는 학생이 아니라 선생님이야." (I am not a student but a teacher.) emphasizes being a teacher and not a student. This type of negative-contrast expression is widely used not only in everyday casual conversations but also in formal explanations or situations where corrections are made.

A 마크 씨는 ***의사가 아니라*** 약사라고 했지?
Mark said he's not a doctor but a pharmacist, right?

B 맞아. 마크 씨는 약사고, 그의 여자 친구인 에밀리 씨가 의사야.
Right. Mark is a pharmacist, and his girlfriend Emily is a doctor.

A 그렇구나. 약사 의사 커플이라니 정말 멋지다!
I see. A pharmacist-doctor couple? That's really cool!

A 친구 생일이에요? 웬 선물을 이렇게 많이 사셨어요?
Is it your friend's birthday? Why did you buy so many gifts?

B ***친구 생일이 아니라*** 친구 부모님 생신이에요. 친부모님처럼 가까운 분들이라 마음 가는 대로 샀더니 선물이 많아졌어요.
It's not my friend's birthday, but my friend's parents' birthday. They're like my own parents, so I bought whatever felt was right and ended up with a lot.

A 이웃 사람은 ***한국 사람이 아니라*** 일본 사람이라던데, 일본 어디에서 왔는지 알아?
I heard the neighbors aren't Korean but Japanese. Do you know where in Japan they're from?

B 도쿄에서 왔다고 들었는데···. 아니야, ***도쿄가 아니라*** 오사카라고 했어.
I heard they're from Tokyo.... No, wait, they are not from Tokyo but from Osaka.

97

MP3 097

-(으)려고

In order to... / Planning to...

〈미생〉(2014)

"시간을 아끼려고 계획을 잘 세우다"와 같은 뜻이 아닌 것은?

Which of the following does not mean the same as "시간을 아끼려고 계획을 잘 세우다"?

ⓐ 시간을 아끼고 계획을 잘 세우다

ⓑ 시간을 아끼기 위해 계획을 잘 세우다

ⓒ 시간을 아낄 수 있게 계획을 잘 세우다

-(으)려고

-(으)려고 is used to express the purpose or intention of an action, or an imminent movement or change in state. It combines with verb stems without a final consonant(batchim), verb stems ending in ㄹ, or the ending -(으)시-. It can convey intention when expressing a plan or desire to perform an action, as in "내일은 일찍 일어나려고 한다." (I plan to wake up early tomorrow.). It also indicates signs of an impending change or an event. For example, the sentence "하늘을 보니 곧 비가 쏟아지려고 한다." (Looking at the sky, it seems like it is about to rain cats and dogs.) describes the likelihood of it raining. It is not used when making requests or commands, but primarily conveys a purpose, plan, intention, or describes an imminent situation.

Action!

A 앞으로도 서류를 쉽게 **찾으려고** 가나다 순으로 정리했습니다.
I organized the documents in Korean alphabetical order so that the paperwork will be easier to try and find in the future.

B 정말 수고 많으셨어요. 덕분에 찾기 훨씬 편해졌어요.
Your efforts are really appreciated. Thanks to you, it's much easier to find things.

A 나는 감기에 걸리지 **않으려고** 손을 항상 깨끗이 씻어.
I always wash my hands thoroughly to try avoid catching a cold.

B 감기뿐만 아니라, 손을 자주 씻는 게 건강을 지키는 데 중요해.
Washing your hands frequently isn't just for colds, it's important for keeping healthy.

A 하늘이 갑자기 어두워졌어.
The sky suddenly turned dark.

B 응, 곧 비가 **쏟아지려고** 해.
Yeah, it looks like it's about to pour.

MP3 098

-아/어도

Even if... / Even though...

〈Mr. 플랑크톤〉 (2024)

다음 중 '피곤해도'와 연결이 잘 되는 표현은 무엇일까요?

Which one of the following expressions best connects with "피곤해도"?

ⓐ 쉴 거야.

ⓑ 일하고 싶어.

ⓒ 일하지 않을 거야.

-아/어도

-아/어도 is a suffix that operates as a connecting ending. It indicates an action will occur or a state will be maintained despite any condition or impediment. It combines not only with verbs but also with adjectives, expressing the assumption or concession of a condition or situation. -아도 is added when the stem ends in 아 or 오; -어도 is added when the stem ends in any other vowel. For example, "피곤해도 일하고 싶어." (Even if I'm tired, I want to work.) expresses the conflicting situation of feeling tired yet wanting to work, while "비싸도 살 거예요." (Even if it's expensive, I'll buy it.) expresses the determination to purchase something despite the high price. This expression is primarily used with a meaning similar to 하지만 (but), applicable not only to actual situations but also to hypothetical ones.

A 오늘 날씨가 너무 더워서 사무실에만 있어야겠어요.
It's so hot today that I'll just have to stay in the office.

B **더워도** 저는 외근을 나가야 해요. 고객과 중요한 약속이 있어서요.
Even if it's hot, I have to step out of the office. You see, I have an important appointment with a client.

A 아이고, 고생이시네요. 외근 가실 때는 물을 충분히 마시고 조심하세요.
Oh dear. Thanks for your hard work. Make sure to drink plenty of water and be careful when you step out of the office.

A 몸살 감기로 몸이 안 좋아. 그런데 **아파도** 마스크를 쓰고 학교에 가야 해. 기말고사라서.
I'm feeling under the weather with a cold. But even if I'm sick, I have to wear a mask and go to school. You see, it's the final exam.

B 이런, 정말 안됐다. 그래도 너무 무리하지 말고, 갔다 와서 푹 쉬어.
Oh dear, I'm so sorry to hear that. Still, don't push yourself too hard. Get a good rest when you get back.

A **늦어도** 좋으니 꼭 전화해. Even if it is late, call me.

B 네, 엄마. 걱정 마세요. 만약 집에 늦게 도착하면 전화 대신 문자 드릴게요.
Yes, mom. Don't worry. If I get home late, I'll text you instead of calling.

MP3 099

-(으)ㄴ/는 대로

As soon as... / According to ...

〈사내맞선〉 (2022)

'학교를 졸업하는 대로 유럽으로 배낭여행을 갈 거예요.'와 같은 뜻이 아닌 것은?

Which one of the following does not have the same meaning as "학교를 졸업하는 대로 유럽으로 배낭여행을 갈 거예요."?

ⓐ 학교를 졸업하자마자 유럽으로 배낭여행을 갈 거예요.

ⓑ 학교를 졸업하기 전에 유럽으로 배낭여행을 갈 거예요.

ⓒ 학교를 졸업한 후에 바로 유럽으로 배낭여행을 갈 거예요.

-(으)ㄴ/는 + 대로 = -(으)ㄴ/는 대로

-(으)ㄴ/는 대로 indicates that one event occurs and is immediately followed by another event in the same state. When the verb stem is in the past tense, use -ㄴ 대로 if it ends in a vowel and -은 대로 if it ends in a consonant. -는 대로 is used when speaking in the present tense. For example, "도착하는 대로 전화해." (Call me as soon as you arrive.) means to call immediately upon arrival, and "말한 대로 진행했어." (I proceeded according to what I said.) indicates that the action was carried out as what was previously stated. This expression emphasizes how one action follows another immediately upon completion, or that an existing state is maintained without change. -자마자 is a similar expression.

A 회의가 **끝나는 대로** 회의록을 바로 이메일로 보내드릴게요.
I'll email you the meeting minutes as soon as the meeting ends.

B 감사합니다. 이메일을 **받는 대로** 나머지 팀원들에게 전달할게요.
Thanks. I'll forward them to the rest of the team as soon as I receive them.

A 내일 시험이 **끝나는 대로** 남자 친구랑 연극 보러 갈 거야.
I'm going to see a play with my boyfriend as soon as my exam ends tomorrow.

B 부럽다. 재미있게 보고 와서 이야기해 줘.
I'm jealous. Have fun and tell me all about it when you get back.

A 리사 씨가 **도착하는 대로** 같이 저녁 먹을 거야.
I'm having dinner with Lisa as soon as she arrives.

B 아, 맞다. 오늘 리사 씨가 부산에서 온다고 했지? 마중 나갈 거야?
Oh, right. You said that Lisa was coming from Busan today, didn't you?
Are you going to go pick her up?

A 응, 청소 끝나자마자 서울역으로 데리러 갈 거야.
Yeah, I'll head to Seoul Station to pick her up as soon as I finish cleaning.

A 요즘 브이로그 찍고 있다고 하지 않았어? 언제쯤 볼 수 있어?
Didn't you say you've been filming vlogs lately? When can we see them?

B 첫 번째 영상은 이미 다 찍었고, 지금 편집하고 있어. 편집이 **끝나는 대로** 바로 올릴 거야!
I already filmed the first video and am editing it now. I'll upload it as soon as the editing is done!

MP3 100

-는 동안에

While doing...

〈월수금화목토〉 (2022)

"여행하는 동안에는 연락하기 힘들 것 같아."는 어떤 의미일까요?

What does "여행하는 동안에는 연락하기 힘들 것 같아." mean?

ⓐ 여행지에 도착하는 대로 연락하겠다.

ⓑ 여행 중에는 연락이 잘 안 될 수 있다.

ⓒ 여행할 때도 평소처럼 자주 연락할 수 있다.

-는 동안 + 에 = -는 동안에

-는 동안(에) indicates when either one action is in in progress or when a certain state persists, another action occurs simultaneously. For example, "내가 요리하는 동안에 너는 설거지해." (While I'm cooking, you do the dishes.) means you should do the dishes during the same time when I cook. -는 is added to the verb stem to indicate the ongoing action, and this is then combined with 동안에 to signify the duration. Depending on the context, it can also describe the time during which a specific state or state continues, not just actions that are simultaneous.

A 내가 **요리하는 동안에** 네가 청소를 끝내야 밥 먹고 둘이 같이 영화 보러 가지.
You need to finish cleaning while I cook so that we can eat and go see a movie together.

B 진짜 청소하기 싫은데…. 영화 보려면 해야지.
I really don't want to clean.... But I guess I have to if I want to see the movie.

A 나 언제까지 기다려야 해?
How long do I have to wait?

B 강아지 **목욕시키는 동안에** 게임 한 판 하고 있어. 끝나자마자 바로 나가자.
Play a game while I wash the dog. Let's head out as soon as I'm done.

A **일하는 동안에** 음악을 듣는 것은 집중력 높이는 데 도움이 돼요.
Listening to music while working helps me focus.

B 저는 반대예요. **일하는 동안에는** 주변이 조용해야 집중이 잘 돼요. 물론, 커피는 필수고요.
I'm the opposite. I concentrate well when working in a quiet surrounding. Of course, coffee is a must.

Meaning & Us
Quiz !?
Action!

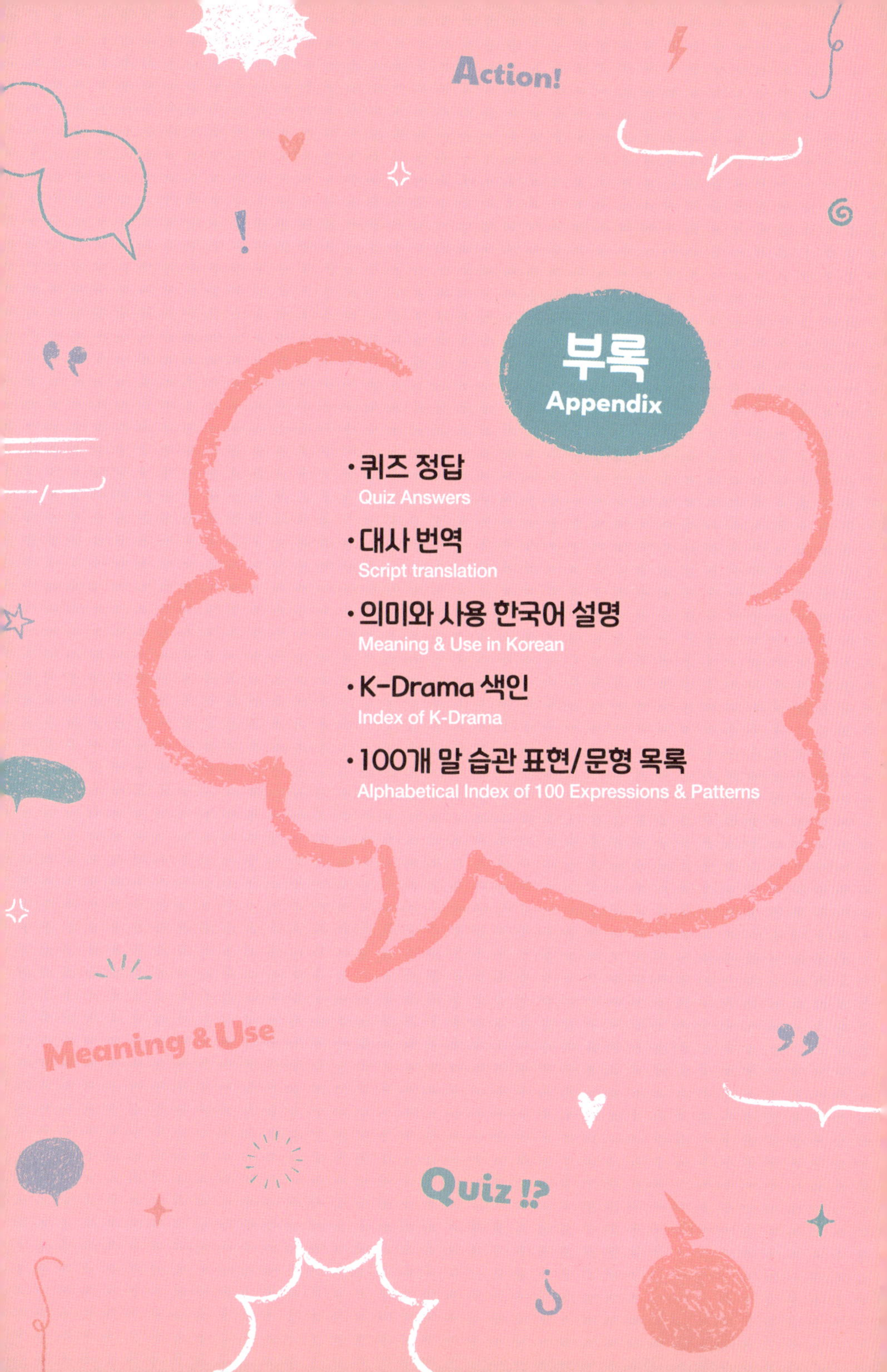

부록
Appendix

- 퀴즈 정답
  Quiz Answers
- 대사 번역
  Script translation
- 의미와 사용 한국어 설명
  Meaning & Use in Korean
- K-Drama 색인
  Index of K-Drama
- 100개 말 습관 표현/문형 목록
  Alphabetical Index of 100 Expressions & Patterns

퀴즈 정답 Quiz Answers

Part 1 말 습관 표현 Speech Expressions

1 있잖아 ⓒ
You know…

2 저기요 ⓒ
Hey there… / Excuse me…

3 미안하지만 / 죄송하지만 ⓑ
Sorry, but…

4 가만히 있어 봐 ⓐ
Hold on / Wait

5 개인적으로 ⓑ
Personally…

6 솔직히 ⓒ
Honestly… / To be honest…

7 아니 ⓐ
No / Uh

8 그러니까 ⓐ, ⓑ, ⓒ
So… / In other words…

9 그런 것 같아 ⓑ
It seems like that… / I guess so…

10 그치? ⓒ
Right? / Isn't it?

11 정말? ⓒ
Really?

12 아깝다 ⓑ
What a shame/waste

13 뭐랄까 ⓒ
How should I put it…

14 대박! ⓒ
Awesome! / Wow!

15 짜증나 ⓒ
I'm annoyed

16 헐 ⓐ
Whoa / Oh my god

17 말도 안돼 ⓐ
No way / Unbelievable

18 그렇긴 한데 ⓒ
That's true, but…

19 완전 ⓑ
Total(ly) / Complete(ly)

20 뭐라고? ⓒ
What did you say?

21 아무튼 ⓑ
At any rate… / Anyway…

22 당연하지 ⓒ
Of course

23 글쎄 ⓒ
Hmm… / Well…

24 어쩌라고? ⓒ
So what?

25 어쩔 수 없지 ⓑ
It is what it is / It can't be helped

26 그렇구나 ⓒ
I see

27 뭔가 ⓒ
Something…

28 지금? ⓒ
Now?

29 설마 ⓒ
No way / You can't be serious

30 혼나다 ⓑ
Almost died…

31 약간 ⓒ
A bit… / Slightly…

32 그거 알지? ⓒ
Do you catch my drift?

33 내가 할게 ⓑ
I'll take care of it / I'll do it

34 그럴 거야 ⓑ
It most likely will… / Probably…

35 뻔하지 ⓒ
I knew it / It's obvious

36 장난 아니야 ⓑ
No joke / Seriously

37 뭐 하자는 거야? ⓑ
What are you trying to do?

38 그만해 ⓒ
That's enough / Stop it

39 당장 ⓒ
Right away / Immediately

40 왜 그래? ⓒ
What's the matter with you?

41 이게 뭐야? ⓐ, ⓑ
What's this?

42 됐어 ⓑ
It's fine / Forget it

43 알았어 ⓐ
Okay / I got it

44 너무해(요) ⓒ
That is too much/so mean/unfair

45 신경 쓰지 마 ⓒ
Don't worry about it

46 -지 뭐 ⓒ
Happens though

47 대충 ⓐ
Roughly / More or less

48 나도 그래 ⓒ
Same here / Me too

49 그냥 ⓐ, ⓑ
Just… / Simply…

50 느낌이 이상해 ⓑ
Something feels off

Part 2 말습관 문형
Speech Patterns

51 같은데 ⓒ
I think / It seems like…

52 -(으)ㄹ 걸? ⓐ
I guess… / Probably…

53 -길래 ⓑ
As… / Because…

54 -(으)ㄴ/는 거 아니야/아니에요? ⓑ
Isn't this…? / Aren't you…?

55 -더라고(요) ⓐ
I noticed/realized...

56 -게 됐어 ⓒ
I ended up… / It turned out…

57 -잖아(요) ⓐ
(I told you/You told me...) right?

58 -고 말았어 ⓐ
I end(ed) up…

59 -는 중이야 ⓒ
I'm in the middle of… / On the way…

60 -나 봐 ⓐ
I guess… / It seems like…

61 -(으)ㄹ래? ⓑ
Do you want to…?

62 -(으)ㄴ/는 것 같아 ⓒ
It seems like… / I think…

63 -게 ⓒ
So that…

64 -(으)ㄹ 뻔했어 ⓒ
I almost (didn't, couldn't, etc)…

65 -(으)ㄹ 테니까 ⓒ
So… / Since…

66 -(으)ㄹ지도 몰라 ⓐ
It might be… / I don't know, maybe…

67 -기만 하면 ⓐ
Whenever… / As long as…

68 -았/었으면 좋겠어 ⓑ
I wish… / I just hope…

69 -(으)ㄹ 거야 ⓒ
I'll make sure… / I'm going to…

70 -았/었더라면 ⓑ
If I had…

71 -지 않을까? ⓒ
Don't you think…? / Maybe it will…

72 -고 나서 ⓑ
Then… / After…

73 -다가 ⓑ
While…

74 -(으)ㄹ 만해 ⓐ
It's worth doing…

75 -자마자 ⓑ
As soon as…

76 -(으)ㄴ/는 편이야 ⓒ
Tend to be…

77 -(으)ㄴ/는 척하다 ⓑ
To pretend…

78 -(으)ㄹ 리가 없어 ⓐ
There's no way…

79 -(으)ㄴ 적 있어? ⓐ
Have you ever…?

80 -는 게 낫지 않아? ⓑ
Isn't it better…?

81 -기도 하고… ⓐ
Also… / Both… and…

82 -(으)ㄹ 수밖에 없어 ⓒ
Can't help… / It's inevitable…

83 -(으)ㄹ 필요가 없어 ⓑ
No need to…

84 -거든(요) ⓒ
Actually…

85 -아/어도 돼? ⓒ
Is it okay/fine…?

86 -기 싫어 ⓐ
To not want to…

87 -았/었어야 했는데 ⓒ
Should have…

88 -더니 ⓐ
As a result…

89 -(으)ㄴ/는가 보다, -나 보다 ⓐ
Looks like… / I guess…

90 -(으)ㄹ까 봐 ⓐ
To be worried/afraid...

91 -기로 했어 ⓒ
Decided to...

92 -는 바람에 ⓐ
Due to... (negative consequence)

93 (-(으)ㄴ/는) 덕분에 ⓑ
Thanks to...

94 -(으)면 할수록 ⓐ
The more ..., the more...

95 -고 싶어(요) ⓒ
Want to...

96 이/가 아니라 ⓑ
It's not... but...

97 -(으)려고 ⓐ
In order to... / Planning to...

98 -아/어도 ⓑ
Even if... / Even though...

99 -(으)ㄴ/는 대로 ⓑ
As soon as... / According to ...

100 -는 동안에 ⓑ
While doing...

대사 번역 Script translation

Part 1 말 습관 표현 Speech Expressions

1 있잖아 You know...

You know, I started crying the moment that projectionist came into the projection room with his tinted glasses on.

2 저기요 Hey there... / Excuse me...

Hey there, I'm sorry that we keep crossing paths like this, but I think we'll have to put up with it since we live in the same neighborhood.

3 미안하지만 / 죄송하지만 Sorry, but...

Man: Do you now fathom how lonely I've been? For 983 years?

Woman: Sorry, but I don't know what loneliness is.

4 가만히 있어 봐 Hold on / Wait

Kiddo, hold on. You got hurt this morning because of me.

5 개인적으로 Personally...

Man: I personally feel very proud of myself for discovering your high potential, Manager Son.

Woman: I will lead the company to become number one in the industry by providing momentum for growth.

6 솔직히 Honestly... / To be honest...

To be honest, I didn't like it. But unlike us, Ms. Sarang just jumped in fervor at the chairman's every word.

7 아니 No / Uh

Uh, who the hell paid our hospital bills?

8 그러니까 So... / In other words...

Man 1: Not just anyone can perform this surgery.

Man 2: So, so I said I would do it (the surgery).

9 그런 것 같아
It seems like that... / I guess so...

Man 1: Am I crying?

Man 2: Um, I guess so.

10 그치? Right? / Isn't it?

Consistent reliability is my charm, right?

11 정말? Really?

Man: I searched the whole neighborhood looking for you.

Woman: Really?

12 아깝다 What a shame/waste

Man 1: Do you not go on things like dates? You're wasting your youth, man.

Man 2: What are you talking about? Why would I go on dates....

13 뭐랄까 How should I put it...

Woman 1: But lately, I feel a bit weird. How should I put it? It's like the feeling of dreaming?

Woman 2: Have you been watching too many dramas again?

14 대박! Awesome! / Wow!

Hey, wow! I've been dying to get a hold of these!

15 짜증나 I'm annoyed

Mr. Hong, aren't you being too harsh? Forget it, I'm not going to drink coffee. I'm annoyed, really.

16 헐 Whoa / Oh my god

Whoa, I moved.

17 말도 안돼 No way / Unbelievable

Wow, no way! Nahee really did it. An athlete of the national team.

18 그렇긴 한데 That's true, but...

Woman 1: Our King Hotel isn't exactly a place where you can come just because of pure luck. Am I correct?

Woman 2: Yes, that's true, but...

19 완전 Total(ly) / Complete(ly)

By the way, isn't your young master a total nut job?

20 뭐라고? What did you say?

Woman: I really want to go home.

Man: What, what did you say?

21 아무튼 At any rate... / Anyway...

Man: I think we should put a sticker on the car. It's better than not being able to find it like this.

Woman: At any rate, no way. Absolutely not.

22 당연하지 Of course

Father: Are you forgiving me?

Son: Of course.

23 글쎄 Hmm... / Well...

Man: Where are we...

Woman: Ah, hmm, I also don't have a clue.

24 어쩌라고? So what?

Man 1: You know what? I guess I really liked Sol a lot.

Man 2: So what? Is this something that concerns me?

25 어쩔 수 없지
It is what it is / It can't be helped

Woman: Looks like it's all sold out now...

Man: Really? Well, it is what it is.

26 그렇구나 I see

Man 1: Hold on a second. Hey, it looks like we are after the same guy!

Man 2: Ah~ I see...!

27 뭔가 Something...

Woman 1: We cut ties.

Woman 2: Cut ties? Um... 'cut ties'... sounds like something... straight out of a book...

28 지금? Now?

Yeah, Grandma. Me, now? I'm going to sightsee.

29 설마 No way / You can't be serious

Woman: Surely there is no way you are actually thinking about marriage...?

30 혼나다 Almost died...

Woman: Why are you laughing?

Man: Because I'm happy. I almost died as I really missed seeing your face last night.

31 약간 A bit... / Slightly...

Woman 1: What happens when an almond dies? "Die, almond."

Man 2: Minjoo Kwon, so your sense of humor leans towards a bit of a lame joke, huh.

32 그거 알지? Do you catch my drift?

Man: What are we going to eat here?

Woman: When you think of the Han River, it's instant noodles. You know for certain, right? The vending machine instant noodles.

33 내가 할게 I'll take care of it / I'll do it

Man: Oh, I'll take care of it. You can call it a day.

Woman: Let's do it together. It'll get done quicker if we work together.

34 그럴 거야 It most likely will… / Probably…

Dosan, you're my beautiful music box. You've comforted me for so long, and it'll most likely will be like that always.

35 뻔하지 I knew it / It's obvious

I know the repertoire though. Grandpa's sacrificing himself for me, so how can I just do what I like?

36 장난 아니야 No joke / Seriously

Woman: Are you feeling under the weather?

Man: Hey, I'm totally fine! No joke.

37 뭐 하자는 거야? What are you trying to do?

Man 1: I'm not waiting for that lovey-dovey.

Man 2: What are you trying to do by saying that to me right now?

38 그만해 That's enough / Stop it

Man: Why won't you give me that kind of a chance? Why can't I do what you did for me?

Woman: That's enough. Stop it.

39 당장 Right away / Immediately

If you are inconvenienced by anything while living here, just let me know anytime. I'll take care of it right away.

40 왜 그래? What's the matter with you?

Man: This parking lot can be used as a space for the guests.

Woman: What in the world is the matter with you? Why are you telling me to sell the car?

41 이게 뭐야? What's this?

Woman: Grandma, what's this?

Grandma: Huh? Oh, that's a flyer I made to hire part-time workers.

42 됐어 It's fine / Forget it

Mom: I'm making fresh kimchi to give you.

Daughter: It's fine. Don't send it. I can just buy it here whenever I need it.

43 알았어 Okay / I got it

Girl: Uncle, if you find out who it is, you have to tell Byuli too. Promise!

Uncle: Yeah, got it. Promise.

44 너무해(요) That is too much/so mean/unfair

Man: Are there trips that allocate no free time?

Woman: Yeah. It's not like we're living under a dictatorship. That's too much.

45 신경 쓰지 마 Don't worry about it

Don't pay attention to what they say.

46 -지 뭐 Happens though

Man: My family is messed up.

Woman: No way. Being messed up is something that happens though when you're young.

47 대충 Roughly / More or less

Man: Um, how about we get the basics done more or less and finish it tomorrow? You haven't even eaten yet.

Woman: Oh, I'm almost done.

48 나도 그래 Same here / Me too

Woman: But. it feels really weird. Being together like this.

Man: Same here.

49 그냥 Just... / Simply...

Man: Get in (the car). I'll take you home.

Woman: Just give me the umbrella and go.

50 느낌이 이상해 Something feels off

Man: Boss? Are you feeling unwell?

Woman: No, it's just that, something feels off.

Part 2 말습관 문형 Speech Patterns

51 같은데 I think / It seems like...

Man: Hmph. Nervous, huh?

Woman: That's rich, coming from someone who got all dressed up from head to toe just to be on TV.

52 -(으)ㄹ 걸? I guess... / Probably...

I probably should've gotten an autograph over here...!

53 -길래 As... / Because...

A middle-aged woman: How could I not be startled when you're standing there like a ghost?

A young woman: I thought there might've been a mistake with the order. Your eyes were half-closed.

54 -(으)ㄴ/는 거 아니야/아니에요? Isn't this...? / Aren't you...?

Woman: What do you want to do? Living hard wasn't your dream, was it?

Man: I'm going to eat jajangmyeon with you at eleven o'clock. Isn't this a victory?

55 -더라고(요) I noticed/realized...

I noticed that my daughter just couldn't study well. Even in elementary school, I realized she spent a whole year memorizing those multiplication tables.

56 -게 됐어 I ended up... / It turned out...

Woman: I'm sorry about the rare earth metals thing...

Man: It's nothing for you to apologize about though, Young-i...

57 -잖아(요) (I told you/You told me...) right?

Woman: Oh, wait—drink this. You don't like sweet things, right?

Man: Thanks.

58 -고 말았어 I end(ed) up...

Woman: I think I need to retrieve my shampoo, my conditioner, and my body wash.

Man: Sorry, but I'll turn down your offer. I ended up coming to the realization that I can't live without Elast-aen now.

59 -는 중이야
I'm in the middle of... / On the way...

Man: Let's talk in person, face to face. Okay?

Woman: I'm on my way to my mom's place.

60 -나 봐 I guess... / It seems like...

Woman 1: Hey, do you have a boyfriend?

Woman 2: I'm trying to get one—dressing up and waiting for his to contact me. He hasn't' come yet. But why...

Woman 1: Guess he's playing hard to get.

61 -(으)ㄹ래? Do you want to...?

Man: Lin, shall we start dating now?

Woman: Huh?

62 -(으)ㄴ/는 것 같아
It seems like... / I think...

Sitting like this, it seems like we are having a formal meeting between our families. Don't you think?

63 -게 So that...

Managing your mental state is part of my job. My job is to help you keep challenging yourselves so that you don't giving up.

64 -(으)ㄹ 뻔했어
I almost (didn't, couldn't, etc)...

By any chance are you Sol? I almost didn't recognize you.

65 -(으)ㄹ 테니까 So... / Since...

I'll hold you from behind, so try riding it slowly once.

66 -(으)ㄹ지도 몰라
It might be... / I don't know, maybe...

To be honest, it might be that your(the vet's) coaching wasn't wrong. Nothing bothers her more than things that come and go.

67 -기만 하면 Whenever... / As long as...

Woman: I wish our Geum-myeong grows up to be the one who doesn't set the table, but instead lives life overturning it.

Man: You overturn it too. Whenever you overturn it, I'll handle everything that follows.

68 -았/었으면 좋겠어 I wish... / I just hope...

Just the thought of competing in the evaluation match makes me a little nervous. It's my first time, you know. I just hope I don't finish last place.

69 -(으)ㄹ 거야
I'll make sure... / I'm going to...

Man: You're going to lose, just you wait. I'll going to make sure you lose. Crying and screaming, dying and living...

Woman: First win, then talk.

70 -았/었더라면 If I had...

If I had only known back then that spring was truly spring, I would've lived differently, more intensely...

71 -지 않을까?
Don't you think...? / Maybe it will...

Man 1: The topic of our presentation started from the point of view that it might be possible to have a critical mind- a question of 'don't you think the subject of recognition is really the subject of denial?'

Man 2: You should catch your breath. Is someone chasing after you?

72 -고 나서 Then... / After...

It was the day of my first game back after the operation on my shoulder. In the end, that game turned out to be my last game.

73 -다가 While...

I've actually won the Brave Citizen Award twice. Once was when I caught a pickpocket while walking down the street...

74 -(으)ㄹ 만해 It's worth doing...

Younger sister: Well, it's worth doing though. Breaks are strict, and but the food is decent.

Older sister: Really?

75 -자마자 As soon as...

Most are operated on as soon as they are born and grow up healthy.

76 -(으)ㄴ/는 편이야 Tend to be...

Woman: It looks like you were reading a book?

Man: I keep books close at hand and I tend to have a deep appreciation for music and art.

77 -(으)ㄴ/는 척하다 To pretend...

Oh my gosh, you startled me! You said to pretend as if we don't know each other at school.

78 -(으)ㄹ 리가 없어 There's no way...

No. There's no way. God wouldn't have given me that ability as a punishment.

79 -(으)ㄴ 적 있어? Have you ever...

Have you ever ridden in a car driven by your friend?

80 -는 게 낫지 않아? Isn't it better...?

If it is hard when you give up and if it is hard when you do not give up, isn't it better to just do what you love and endure the hardship?

81 -기도 하고··· Also... / Both... and...

Woman 1: (About casting) There's no desperation.

Woman 2: Yeah, I sometimes get hung up while I'm working, because I feel that the work I've done is at a waste. I feel it is also desperation. But I don't feel this way before I start. I hate that feeling of losing from the start, so I just don't get caught up in it.

82 -(으)ㄹ 수밖에 없어 Can't help... / It's inevitable...

I can't help but like you.

83 -(으)ㄹ 필요가 없어 No need to...

Didn't I tell you? There is no need to call me out separately. I'll be there first on my own on the day that jajangmyeon(Korean black bean noodles) is served.

84 -거든(요) Actually...

It's quite fascinating. I'm actually your fan. I've watched every single one of your games. Because I want to be like you..

85 -아/어도 돼? Is it okay/fine...?

Man 1: Hey, you! What the hell is wrong with you? Is it okay for you to make someone do something like that?

Man 2: You can say that again.

86 -기 싫어 To not want to...

Woman 1: I don't want to doubt you. Seriously, you never liked him, did you?

Woman 2: No.

87 -았/었어야 했는데 Should have...

Old man: I'm sorry.

Man: Why are you apologizing, sir?

Old man: I think it's my fault. I should have been the one who got injured instead...

88 -더니 As a result...

Man 1: Lately I've been able to sleep in the early morning, thanks to Yeonsu.

Man 2: You didn't listen when I was talking. But you listen to what Yeonsu says, huh?

89 -(으)ㄴ/는가 보다, -나 보다 Looks like... / I guess...

Man 1: So it looks like a family of three?

Man 2: Yes, a family of three.

90 -(으)ㄹ까 봐 To be worried/afraid...

I was going crazy as a result of thinking. I was worried I wouldn't see any of the three. But I feel much better after seeing the poems before I leave. I feel so much butter. In the next life, I'll listen to five or ten of them.

91 -기로 했어 Decided to...

Woman: Um, I've decided to take up Mr. Jang, Jang Baek-gi's advice.

Man: Huh?

Woman: I've decided to lose, just like Mr. Baekgi said. I realized that the way to defeat a strong spear isn't with a stronger shield or spear.

92 -는 바람에 Due to... (negative consequence)

Man 1: Someone from your department spilled glue all over the documents and due to that someone from my department got scolded!!

Man 2: What did someone (from my department) do?

93 (-(으)ㄴ/는) 덕분에 Thanks to...

It feels as if I woke up from a dream. I never imagined I'd be able to go on a trip abroad, but thanks to you, I got to see another country. I'm so grateful today.

94 -(으)면 할수록 The more ..., the more...

Man: Why are you laughing like that?

Woman: The more I think about it, the more funnier it gets. Its the first time I see someone ring a golden bell at a snack bar in my life.

95 -고 싶어(요) Want to...

I want to be on the same side as the lawyer.

96 이/가 아니라 It's not... but...

Woman 1: Team Leader Jin, why do you keep buying clothes that copy others?

Woman 2: It's not who is copying others, but you, director.

97 -(으)려고 In order to... / Planning to...

If you lack the skill, they'll use that to try to make themselves look good. Even if you're skilled, they'll use that to make themselves look good.

98 -아/어도 Even if... / Even though...

Man: Don't go.

Woman: It's no use crying over spilt milk. I'll go even if you hold me back.

99 -(으)ㄴ/는 대로 As soon as... / According to ...

I'll pay off the hospital bills as soon as I get my paycheck.

100 -는 동안에 While doing...

I entered my 30s as I became a veteran in the field over the course of 13-years.

의미와 사용 한국어 설명 Meaning & Use in Korean

Part 1 말 습관 표현
Speech Expressions

1 있잖아
You know...

'있잖아'는 '있다'와 '잖아'가 합쳐진 표현으로, 듣는 사람이 이미 알고 있는 사실을 전제로 주의를 끌거나 이야기를 시작할 때 사용합니다. 비슷한 표현으로는 '아니, 그게…', '저기…' 등이 있으며, 중요한 이야기를 꺼내기 전 상대방의 관심을 집중시키는 역할을 합니다. '네가 했잖아.', '춥잖아.'처럼 '-잖아'를 문장 끝에 쓰면 이미 알고 있는 사실을 확인하거나 강조하는 뉘앙스를 주고, '있잖아'를 문두에 단독으로 쓰면 '내 말 좀 들어 봐.'처럼 청자의 주의를 환기시키는 기능이 강합니다. 특히 로맨틱한 고백 장면에서 자주 쓰이며, 바로 말하기 부끄러운 마음을 전하기 전에 '있잖아'로 상대방의 시선을 끌고 이어서 '너를 좋아해.', '사랑해.'처럼 속마음을 전하는 흐름으로 쓰입니다.

2 저기요
Hey there... / Excuse me...

'저기요'는 잘 모르는 상대를 부를 때 쓰는 말로 주로 낯선 사람이나 서비스업 종사자의 주의를 끌기 위해 사용하는 공손한 표현입니다. 길을 물어볼 때나 식당에서 종업원을 부를 때와 같은 공공장소에서, 비슷한 나이나 자신보다 어린 상대에게 자주 쓰입니다. 누군가를 부르거나 어떤 것을 지적할 때, 혹은 대화를 시작할 때도 유용하며, 특히 상대방의 이름을 모르거나 적절한 호칭이 떠오르지 않을 때 효과적으로 활용됩니다. 비슷한 표현으로는 '저', '실례합니다', '여기요' 등이 있으며, '잠시만요', '잠깐만요'처럼 양해를 구하며 주의를 끄는 말도 자주 사용됩니다. 한편, '저기'는 '저기요'보다 덜 공식적인 표현으로, 주로 친구나 동료처럼 가까운 사이에서 주의를 끌거나 대화를 시작할 때 사용하며, 상대방의 이름이나 호칭이 바로 떠오르지 않을 때도 유용합니다.

3 미안하지만 / 죄송하지만
Sorry, but...

'미안하지만'과 '죄송하지만'은 상대방에 대해 마음이 편치 못하고 부끄러운 감정을 표현하는 '미안'과, 더 정중하게 죄스러운 마음을 드러내는 '죄송'에 접속 부사 '하지만'이 결합한 표현입니다. '하지만'은 서로 상반되는 사실을 이어 주는 기능을 합니다. 이 표현은 도움을 요청하거나, 거절하거나, 민감한 대화를 시작할 때 말투를 부드럽게 하고 상대의 기분을 배려하기 위하여 자주 사용됩니다. '미안하지만'은 반말 상황에서 쓰이며, '죄송하지만'은 존댓말 상황에서 사용됩니다. 유사한 표현으로는 '미안한데', '미안합니다만', '죄송합니다만', '실례지만' 등이 있습니다.

4 가만히 있어 봐
Hold on / Wait

'가만히'는 '아무 말이나 움직임 없이 조용히'라는 뜻이며, '있다'와 결합하여 '아무런 행동을 하지 않고 그대로 있는 것'을 나타냅니다. 여기에 '-아/어 봐'가 붙어 '가만히 있어 봐'는 상대방에게 잠시 기다리거나 조용히 있어 달라고 요청하는 표현이 됩니다. 이 말은 주로 친구나 가족 등 가까운 관계에서 사용되며, 어떤 상황을 정리하거나 무언가에 집중하기 위해 자주 쓰입니다. 또한 깊이 생각할 시간이 필요할 때도 활용됩니다. 상대방의 말이나 행동이 방해가 될 때 다소 짜증 섞인 어투로 쓰이는 경우도 많습니다. 예를 들어, '정신 사나우니까 가만히 좀 있어 봐.'와 같이 말할 수 있으며, 유사한 표현으로는 '잠깐만', '기다려 봐', '잠시만' 등이 있습니다.

5 개인적으로
Personally...

'개인적으로'는 '자신과 직접 관련되게, 또는 자신의 입장에서'라는 뜻을 가진 부사입니다. 이 표현은 어떤 주제에 대해 화자가 자신의 생각이나 관점을 밝히거나, 상대에게 조언을 건넬 때 자주 사용됩니다. 뒤에 이어지는 내용은 일반적이거나 객관적인 의견이 아니라 화자의 주관적인 판단임을 전제로 하며, 이를 통해 '이건 어디까지나 내 생각이다'라는 뉘앙스를 전달할 수 있습니다. 비슷한 표현으로는 '내 생각에는', '내 입장은' 등이 있습니다.

6 솔직히

Honestly... / To be honest...

'솔직히'는 '숨김이나 거짓이 없이 바르고 곧게'라는 뜻을 가진 말입니다. 구어에서는 '솔직히 말하면'의 줄임말로 쓰이며, 화자가 자신의 생각이나 사실을 숨기지 않고 드러내고자 할 때 사용됩니다. 특히 개인적이거나 민감한 상황에서 의견을 밝히거나, 고백·비판·칭찬을 할 때 자주 활용됩니다. 또한 대화의 분위기를 전환하며 중요한 이야기를 꺼낼 때 효과적으로 쓰이기도 합니다. 비슷한 표현으로는 '사실은', '진짜로',인터넷과 SNS에서 자주 쓰이는 '찐으로', 그리고 '솔직히 까놓고 말해서'의 줄임말인 '솔까말' 등이 있습니다.

7 아니

No / Uh

'아니'는 본래 '그렇지 않다'라는 뜻으로 상대방의 말이나 질문을 부정할 때 쓰이지만, 구어에서는 뜻밖의 상황에 놀라거나 감탄을 표현하는 감탄사로도 자주 사용됩니다. 예를 들어 '벌써 자니?'라는 물음에 '아니, 아직 안 자.'라고 답할 수 있고, '아니, 세상에 이런 일이!'처럼 놀라움을 드러낼 수도 있습니다. 또한 비격식적인 대화에서는 다음 말을 꺼내기 전 시간을 벌거나 주의를 끌기 위해 쓰이며, 이때는 주로 '근데'와 결합해 '아니, 근데 말이야···'와 같이 나타나 뒤에 오는 말을 강조하는 기능을 합니다. 더 나아가 '저 집 월세가 30만 원, 아니 10만 원이라 해도 살고 싶지 않다.'처럼 문장이나 명사 사이에서 앞의 내용을 수정하거나 강조하는 용법으로도 활용됩니다.

8 그러니까

So... / In other words...

'그러니까'는 '그런 이유로', '다시 말해서'라는 뜻으로, 앞의 말이 뒤의 말의 근거가 됨을 나타냅니다. 더 명확한 설명을 하거나 간단히 요약할 때, 또는 중요한 점을 강조하고 싶을 때 자주 쓰입니다. 또한 자신이 상대방의 말을 제대로 이해했는지 확인하려고 '그러니까 네 말은···'처럼 말문을 열 때도 사용됩니다. 이 밖에 '이 바지 너무 크지 않아?' – '그러니까.'처럼 상대방의 말에 대한 동의나 공감을 나타낼 때도 쓰이며, 이 경우 '맞아.', '그러게 말이다.'와 비슷한 의미를 가집니다.

9 그런 것 같아

It seems like that... / I guess so...

'그런 것 같아'는 자신이 직접 관찰하거나 들은 정보를 바탕으로, 확정적이지는 않지만 어느 정도 가능성이 높다고 판단될 때 쓰는 표현입니다. 단정적으로 말하지 않으면서도 상대방과 의견을 공유하거나 부드럽게 동의할 때 자주 사용됩니다. 상황에 따라 사실 여부를 조심스럽게 추측하는 뉘앙스를 줄 수도 있고, 대화를 원만하게 이어가기 위한 완충 역할을 하기도 합니다. 특히 의견 차이를 최소화하거나 상대방의 말에 부드럽게 호응할 때 효과적입니다. 비슷한 표현으로는 '그럴 수도 있어.'처럼 가능성을 인정하는 말, '맞는 것 같아.'처럼 타당성을 긍정하는 말이 있습니다.

10 그치?

Right? / Isn't it?

'그치'는 '그렇지'의 준말로, 사실이 그러함을 인정하거나 동의할 때 하는 말입니다. 듣는 사람에게 동의를 구하거나 자신의 말이 맞는지 확인할 때 사용됩니다. 주로 친구나 동료처럼 가까운 관계에서 비격식적으로 쓰이고, 서로 공유한 경험이나 의견을 강조하거나 확인하는 데 자주 활용됩니다. 또한 '그렇지 않아?'를 줄여 '그치 않아?'처럼 쓰이기도 하며, 상황에 따라 가벼운 공감 확인, 사실 여부 점검, 장난스러운 확인 등 다양한 뉘앙스를 담을 수 있습니다. 비슷한 표현으로는 구어·일상에서 쓰이는 '그죠?', '그렇지 않아요?', '맞죠?'가 있으며, 인터넷과 SNS에서는 'ㅇㅈ?(=인정?)', 'ㄹㅇ?(=레알?)'과 같은 축약형 속어로도 쓰입니다. 또한 '아닌가?'처럼 반문 형태로 부드럽게 확인하는 말과도 기능이 통합니다.

11 정말?

Really?

'정말?'은 거짓이 아니고 사실인지를 묻는 의문형 표현으로, 놀람, 불신, 또는 사실 확인의 의미로 사용되는 표현입니다. 상황에 따라 흥분된 톤, 회의적인 톤, 혹은 중립적인 톤으로 쓸 수 있으며, 질문 형식을 띠지만 대체로 상대방의 대답을 꼭 요구하지 않는 수사적 질문으로 사용됩니다. 비슷한 표현으로는 조금 더 구어적이고 친근한 표현인 '진짜?'가 있습니다. 또한 '정말'은 질문이 아닌 문장에서 의미를 강조하는 역할을 하기도 합니다. 예를 들어 '내년에는 정말 국내 여행이라도 한 번 갔으면 좋겠어', '신부가 정말 눈부시게 아름답다'처럼, 감정이나 사실의 강도를 높일 때 사용됩니다. 이와 유사한 '정말로?'라는 표현도 있는데, 두 표현은 비슷하게 쓰이지만 '정말로?'는 주로 믿기 어려운 사실을 확인할 때 더 자주 사용됩니다.

12 아깝다

What a shame/waste

'아깝다'는 '일이 뜻대로 되지 않아 섭섭하고 안타깝거나, 가치 있는 것을 잃거나 쓰기에 섭섭하다'는 뜻을 가진 말입니다. 소중한 것을 잃거나 기회를 놓쳤을 때 느끼는 아쉬움과 안타까움을 나타내며 주로 시간, 돈, 노력, 기회 등이 헛되이 낭비되었을 때 사용됩니다. 또한 게임에서 근소한 차이로 지거나, 무언가를 거의 다 해냈는데 마지막 순간에 실패했을 때도 자주 쓰입니다. 비슷해 보이지만 의미가 다른 표현으로는 '안타깝다'와 '아쉽다'가 있습니다. '안타깝다'는 일이 뜻대로 되지 않거나 보기에 딱해서 가슴이 아픈 감정을 표현하며, '안타깝게도'라고 하면 '불행히도'라는 의미로 쓰입니다. 반면 '아쉽다'는 필요할 때 없거나 모자라 만족스럽지 못하거나, 미련이 남아 서운한 감정을 표현하는데, 예를 들어 '비빔밥에 계란이 빠져서 아쉽네.'처럼 가벼운 상황에서도 사용할 수 있습니다.

13 뭐랄까

How should I put it…

'뭐랄까'는 '뭐라고 할까'의 줄임말로, 말로 표현하기가 어렵거나 적절한 말을 찾기 힘들 때 사용하는 표현입니다. 잠시 생각을 정리할 시간을 벌거나, 쉽게 설명하기 어려운 생각이나 느낌을 전할 때 쓰입니다. 변형 표현으로는 '뭐라고 해야 할까', '뭐라고 하면 좋을까', '뭐라 하지…' 등이 있습니다.

14 대박

Awesome! / Wow!

'대박!'은 어떤 일이 크게 이루어졌음을 비유적으로 나타내는 말로, 예상치 못한 사건이나 놀라운 결과에 대한 놀람·감탄·흥분을 표현할 때 사용되는 속어입니다. 주로 비격식적인 상황에서 쓰이며, 말하는 사람의 어조나 표정에 따라 긍정적인 상황뿐 아니라 부정적인 상황에도 사용될 수 있습니다. '대박이다', '대박 사건'처럼 형태를 변형해 쓰이기도 하며, 비슷한 표현으로는 '와, 대단하다!', '우와' 등이 있습니다. 단순한 놀람을 표현할 때는 '헐', '진짜?' 같은 속어도 자주 사용됩니다.

15 짜증나

I'm annoyed

'짜증나다'는 '마음에 차지 않아 불만스럽고 화가 치밀다'라는 뜻을 가진 말입니다. 구어에서는 주로 '짜증나'의 형태로 줄여 쓰이며, 비격식적인 상황에서 불만·화·답답함을 표현할 때 사용됩니다. 일이 마음대로 되지 않거나 방해를 받을 때, 혹은 상대방의 언행이나 상황이 못마땅할 때 자주 쓰입니다. 자신의 기분이 나쁘다는 것을 강조하고 싶을 때는 '짜증난다고!'라고 할 수 있고, 누군가에게 불만을 직접적으로 표현할 때는 '정말 짜증나게 왜 이래?'처럼 쓸 수 있습니다. 또한 일이 원하는 대로 풀리지 않을 때 혼잣말로도 자주 쓰이며, 주로 친구나 가까운 사이에서 많이 사용됩니다. 비슷한 표현으로는 '화나', '열받아'가 있습니다.

16 헐

Whoa / Oh my god

'헐'은 비격식적인 대화에서 사용하는 감탄사로, 어이없거나 황당해서 맥이 빠질 때, 놀랍거나 충격적인 상황을 접했을 때, 또는 믿기 어려운 사실이나 장면을 목격하거나 들었을 때 쓰입니다. 긍정적인 상황과 부정적인 상황 모두에서 사용할 수 있으며, 때로는 '대박'과 결합해 '헐, 대박.'처럼 감정을 더 강하게 표현하기도 합니다. 비슷한 표현으로는 '와', '진짜?' 등이 있습니다.

17 말도 안 돼

No way / Unbelievable

'말도 안 되다'는 '사리에 맞지 않거나 이치에 맞지 않다'라는 뜻을 가진 말입니다. 구어에서는 주로 '말도 안 돼'라는 감탄형으로 쓰이며, 상대의 말이나 상황이 믿기지 않거나 놀랍다는 것을 표현할 때 사용됩니다. 긍정적이든 부정적이든 예상치 못한 상황에서 충격이나 의심을 나타내는 반응으로 자주 쓰입니다. 뜻밖의 좋은 결과를 얻었을 때나 경기에서 극적인 승리를 거뒀을 때, 또는 이해되지 않는 상황이나 황당한 소식을 들었을 때 자연스럽게 사용됩니다. 비슷한 표현으로는 '진짜?', '세상에!', '거짓말!' 등이 있습니다.

18 그렇긴 한데

That's true, but…

'그렇긴 하다'는 '상대방의 말이나 어떤 사실을 인정하면서도 그에 대해 완전히 동의하지 않고 다른 관점이나 조건을 덧붙이다'라는 뜻을 가진 표현입니다. 구어에서는 '그렇긴 한데'라는 형태로 자주 쓰이며, 상대방의 의견이나 사실을 인정하면서도 부드럽게 다른 의견을 제시할 때 사용됩니다. 사실임을 받아들이면서 대조되는 내용을 덧붙이거나, 반박을 완화하고 조심스럽게 피드백을 전할 때 효과적입니다. 또한 강하게 불만을 표하는 사람을 달래거나 상황을 완화하려는 맥락에서도 쓰입니다. 비슷한 표현으로는 '맞긴 한데', '그렇지, 그런데…' 등이 있습니다.

19 완전

Total(ly) / Complete(ly)

'완전'은 '모자람이나 흠이 없이 모두 갖추어져 있음'을 뜻하는 말입니다. 구어에서는 본래의 의미에서 확장되어 무언가를 강하게 강조할 때 쓰이는 비격식적인 표현으로 자리잡았습니다. 주로 친구나 가까운 사이에서 감탄이나 의견을 힘주어 전하고 싶을 때 사용되며, 긍정적인 상황과 부정적인 상황 모두에서 활용됩니다. 특히 개인적인 기호나 감정을 드러낼 때 자주 등장합니다. 다만 격식 있는 상황이나 공식 문서에서는 '정말', '아주', '매우' 같은 표현으로 바꿔 쓰는 것이 적절합니다. 비슷한 비격식 표현으로는 '진짜', '엄청' 등이 있습니다.

20 뭐라고?

What did you say?

'뭐라고?'는 상대방이 한 말을 다시 물을 때 쓰는 말로 상대방의 말을 잘 듣지 못했거나 믿기 어려운 말을 들었을 때 다시 확인하려는 의도로 사용됩니다. 단순히 내용을 확인하려는 상황에서도 쓰이지만, 말하는 어조와 표정에 따라 의미가 달라집니다. 놀란 표정과 함께 쓰면 상대방의 말을 도저히 믿기 힘들다는 반응이 되고, 화난 어조로 쓰면 상대방이 해서는 안 될 말을 했다는 꾸짖음의 의미가 됩니다. 이와 비슷한 표현으로는 '뭐?', '다시 말해 봐.'가 있으며, 보다 차분하게 발언의 의미나 의도를 확인하고 싶을 때는 '무슨 말이야?'라고 말해 상대의 설명을 구체적으로 요구할 수 있습니다.

21 아무튼

At any rate… / Anyway…

'아무튼'은 '상황이 어떻든'이라는 뜻으로, 앞서 언급된 세부 사항을 더 이상 따지지 않고 결론만 정리하거나 대화를 마무리할 때 쓰는 비격식적인 표현입니다. 듣는 사람에게 '조건과 상관없이 결과는 같다'는 뉘앙스를 전달하며, 가볍게 화제를 전환할 때도 자주 활용됩니다. 비슷한 표현으로는 '어쨌든', '하여튼', '그건 그렇고' 등이 있습니다. 여기에 덧붙여, '그건 그렇고'는 앞서 하던 이야기를 잠시 접고 새로운 주제로 자연스럽게 넘어갈 때 쓰는 표현입니다. 대화의 흐름을 무리 없이 이어가면서도 화제를 전환하는 효과가 있으며, 사소한 안부를 묻거나 중요한 주제로 상대의 주의를 끌 때도 유용합니다. 비슷한 표현으로는 '그런데', '참, 그런데 말이야'가 있습니다.

22 당연하지

Of course

'당연하다'는 '그럴 수 밖에 없어 조금도 이상하지 아니하다'라는 뜻을 가진 말이며, 구어에서는 '당연하지'의 형태로 강한 동의나 확신을 표현할 때 사용됩니다. 상대방의 말이나 제안에 전적으로 동의하거나, 그 내용이 너무나 명확하고 의심할 여지가 없음을 강조하는 기능을 합니다. 상황에 따라 단순한 사실 확인, 격려, 또는 친근한 장난 섞인 동의의 의미를 담을 수 있으며, 주로 친구나 가족 같은 가까운 사이에서 비격식적으로 쓰입니다. 어조에 따라 진지하게도, 가볍게도 전달될 수 있습니다. 비슷한 표현으로는 '물론이지', '그럼'이 있으며, 발음의 유사성을 활용한 변형 표현으로 '당근이지'나 줄임말 '당근'이 널리 쓰여 유쾌하고 친근한 분위기를 만드는 데 자주 활용됩니다.

23 글쎄

Hmm… / Well…

'글쎄'는 '상대방의 질문에 대해 선뜻 긍정이나 부정을 하지 못할 때 내는 소리'라는 뜻을 가진 말입니다. 구어에서는 질문에 즉각적으로 답하기 망설여지거나 다른 사람의 말에 바로 동의하지 않을 때 쓰이며, 일상 대화에서 확신이 없거나 조금 더 생각할 시간이 필요할 때 자주 사용됩니다. 비슷한 표현으로는 '잘 모르겠는데', '음…' 등이 있습니다. 특별한 의미 없이 문장을 매끄럽게 잇기 위해 쓰이기도 하는데, '아니, 글쎄'처럼 쓰면 새로운 이야기를 꺼내며 상대방의 주의를 끌고 호기심을 유도하는 효과를 냅니다.

24 어쩌라고?

So what?

'어쩌다'는 '어떤 일이 우연히 이루어지거나 생기다'라는 뜻을 가진 동사에서 비롯된 말로, '어쩌라고?'는 직역하면 '어떻게 하라고 하느냐'라는 의미가 됩니다. 구어에서는 주로 상대방의 말이나 행동에 짜증, 반항심, 또는 무관심을 드러내는 비격식적인 표현으로 쓰입니다. 보통 상대의 말이 불필요하거나 상황과 직접적인 관련이 없다고 느껴질 때, 혹은 조언이나 간섭이 지나치다고 생각될 때 사용됩니다. 어조에 따라 가벼운 장난처럼 들리기도 하지만, 대부분은 날카롭거나 차가운 인상을 주기 때문에 관계와 상황에 주의해야 합니다. '아, 어쩌라고?', '그래서 뭐 어쩌라고?'처럼 변형해서 쓰이며, 때로는 '네 말이 맞든 틀리든 상관없다'는 태도를 드러내는 말투로도 사용됩니다.

25 어쩔 수 없지

It is what it is / It can't be helped

'어쩔 수 없어'와 '어쩔 수 없지'는 피할 수 없는 상황을 받아들이며 다른 선택의 여지가 없음을 나타내는 표현입니다. 두 표현 모두 의미는 같지만, '어쩔 수 없어'는 혼잣말이나 스스로 상황을 정리하며 받아들일 때 더 자주 쓰이고, '어쩔 수 없지'는 대화 속에서 상대방의 말에 동의하거나 함께 상황을 인정할 때 더 자연스럽게 사용됩니다. 계획이 틀어지거나 기대한 대로 되지 않았을 때, 더 이상 방법이 없음을 인정하며 체념하거나 이해하는 마음을 전할 수 있고, 누군가 좋지 않은 일을 겪었을 때는 '그럴 수도 있으니 너무 자책하지 말라'는 위로의 의미로도 쓰입니다. 또한 이상적으로는 바꾸고 싶지만 현실적으로 불가능하거나 이미 결정된 상황임을 받아들일 때도 사용됩니다. 과거형인 '어쩔 수 없었어/없었지'는 자신이 선택의 여지가 없었다는 점을 강조하며 변명이나 설명의 의미로 쓰일 수 있습니다. 비슷한 표현으로는 '할 수 없어'와 '방법이 없어'가 있습니다.

26 그렇구나

I see

'그렇구나'는 상대방의 말에 공감하거나 이해, 깨달음을 나타낼 때 쓰는 표현으로, 새로운 정보를 들었을 때 자연스럽게 반응하는 일상적인 말입니다. 듣는 사람이 '아, 이제 알겠다'는 의미를 전하며 대화를 부드럽게 이어 주는 역할을 합니다. 그러나 친구들끼리의 비격식적인 대화에서는 꼭 진지하게 이해하거나 깨달았다는 의미가 아니라, 가볍게 받아치거나 장난을 치기 위해 빈정대는 어조로 사용되기도 합니다. 억양과 표정에 따라 따뜻하게 공감하는 뉘앙스가 될 수도 있고, 반대로 비꼬는 뉘앙스가 될 수도 있어 상황에 맞게 주의해서 사용해야 합니다. 과거형으로 표현한 '그랬구나'를 사용하면 상대를 이해한다는 뉘앙스가 더 강하게 전달될 수 있습니다. 비슷한 표현으로는 '아, 그래?', '아, 그렇지'가 있으며, 모두 대화에서 상대방의 말을 받으며 호응하는 기능을 합니다.

27 뭔가

Something…

'뭔가'는 '무엇인가' 또는 '무언가'의 줄임말로, 일상 대화에서 매우 자주 쓰입니다. 주로 불확실하거나 특정되지 않은 대상을 가리킬 때, 혹은 정확히 알지 못하지만 어떤 느낌이나 상태를 표현하고 싶을 때 사용됩니다. 정체를 확신할 수 없을 때의 추측, 그리고 완성도나 상태가 명확히 규정되지 않는 모호한 상황을 묘사하는 데에도 쓰입니다. 비슷한 표현으로 이유는 설명하기 어렵지만 그런 기분이 든다는 뜻의 '왠지', 그리고 정확히는 모르지만 그런 것 같다고 말할 때 쓰는 '뭔지 모르겠지만'이 있습니다.

28 지금?

Now?

'지금'은 '말하는 바로 이때'를 뜻하는 부사입니다. 구어에서는 '지금?'이라는 짧은 의문문 형태로 자주 쓰이며, 현재 즉시 일어나고 있는 행동이나 사건에 대해 확인하거나 반응할 때, 예상치 못한 시점이나 상황에 놀람이나 긴급함을 강조할 때, 난감함·당황스러움·부정적인 감정을 담아 표현할 때 사용됩니다. 억양과 말투에 따라 친근한 되물음부터 강한 당혹감까지 다양한 의미를 전달합니다. 비슷한 표현으로는 '지금 바로?', '당장?'등이 있습니다.

29 설마

No way / You can't be serious

'설마'는 '그럴 리가 있겠느냐 하고 의심하거나 아니라고 단정할 때' 쓰는 표현으로, 구어에서 놀람·불신·당황을 나타낼 때 자주 사용됩니다. 예상치 못한 정보나 믿기 어려운 일을 들었을 때, 가능성을 낮게 보면서도 혹시나 하는 마음을 담을 때, 상대의 말이 장난이나 과장일 것 같다고 느낄 때 활용됩니다. 말투와 억양에 따라 가벼운 농담부터 진지한 부정까지 다양한 뉘앙스를 줄 수 있습니다. 비슷한 표현으로는 '그럴 리가 없어'가 있는데, '설마'가 가능성을 거의 배제하면서도 약간의 여운을 두는 반면, '그럴 리가'는 이치상 불가능함을 강하게 단정하는 표현입니다. 예를 들어, '설마, 네가 그걸 잊었어?'는 '정말 그럴까?'라는 의심과 놀람을 함께 담고 있는 반면, '그럴 리가 없어!'는 사실 자체를 전면적으로 부정하는 말입니다. 두 표현은 모두 믿기 어려운 상황에 반응할 때 쓰이지만, 강도와 어감의 차이가 있습니다.

30 혼나다

Almost died...

'혼이 나다'는 '사람이 무척 놀라거나 당혹스러울 정도로 된통 당하다는 뜻으로 '-아/어서 혼나다'는 어떤 일을 겪으며 무척 힘들거나 고생한 상황을 강조할 때 사용됩니다. '혼꾸멍나다', '혼쭐이 나다'와 같은 말과도 통합니다. 일상에서는 '감기에 걸려서 혼났어.', '더워서 혼났어.', '짜증나서 혼났어.'처럼 육체적·정신적으로 크게 힘들었던 경험을 표현할 때 쓰입니다. 단순히 '힘들었어.'라고 말하는 것보다 훨씬 강하게, 그리고 과장되게 들려 듣는 사람으로 하여금 그 상황을 쉽게 공감하도록 만듭니다.

31 약간

A bit... / Slightly...

'약간'은 정도가 작거나 강하지 않음을 나타낼 때 사용하는 표현입니다. 설명을 부드럽게 하거나 미묘한 차이를 전달할 때도 자주 쓰며, 특히 평가 상황에서는 직접적이거나 강한 인상을 줄 수 있는 표현을 완화하는 역할을 합니다. 이 경우 화자의 태도나 주관적인 느낌이 함께 전달되어, 강한 비판 대신 은근한 의견이나 부드러운 평가를 나타낼 수 있습니다. 번형된 표현으로는 '조금', '살짝' 등이 있습니다.

32 그거 알지?

Do you catch my drift?

'알다'는 '사물이나 사실을 인식하거나 기억하다'라는 뜻을 가진 동사입니다. 구어에서 '그거 알지?'는 주로 화자가 청자도 이미 알고 있을 것이라 가정하고 사실이나 경험을 확인할 때 사용됩니다. 또한 새로운 주제를 꺼내며 청자의 관심을 끌고 화제를 부드럽게 전환하는 기능도 합니다. 억양과 상황에 따라 친근한 확인, 장난스러운 추궁, 진지한 확인 등 다양한 뉘앙스를 담을 수 있습니다. 비슷한 표현으로는 '그거 알아?', '그거 기억나?' 등이 있습니다. 질문형 '그거 알지?'와 달리, 맞장구를 칠 때는 '알지'라고 답하여 상대방의 말에 공감하거나 동의하는 표현으로 쓰입니다. '맞아'와 비슷한 기능으로 대화의 흐름을 자연스럽게 이어 줍니다.

33 내가 할게

I'll take care of it / I'll do it

'내가 할게'는 자신이 책임을 지겠다는 의지나 결단을 나타낼 때 사용합니다. 주로 비격식적인 상황에서 쓰이며, 실제 대화에서는 '할게'를 생략하고 단순히 '내가!' 또는 '내!'라고만 말해도 같은 의미를 전달할 수 있습니다. 이렇게 줄여 쓰면 말의 속도가 빨라지고, 상황에 따라 자신감이나 적극성을 더 강하게 드러낼 수 있습니다. 특히 서로 맥락을 잘 아는 관계에서는 뒤에 술어를 생략해도 의미가 충분히 전달됩니다. 비슷한 표현으로는 '내가 맡을게.', '내가 처리할게.' 등이 있습니다.

34 그럴 거야

It most likely will... / Probably...

'그럴 거야'는 어떤 사실이나 상황에 대해 가능성이나 추측을 나타내는 표현입니다. 확실하지 않지만, 화자가 일정한 믿음을 가지고 있거나 동의하는 뉘앙스를 전할 때 사용합니다. 주로 일상적인 대화에서 가볍게 쓰이며, 말투나 억양에 따라 확신의 정도를 조절할 수 있습니다. 부드러운 억양으로 말하면 조심스러운 추측이 되고, 단호한 억양으로 말하면 강한 확신처럼 들릴 수 있습니다. 변형 표현으로는 '아마 그럴 걸', '그럴 수도 있어' 등이 있습니다.

35 뻔하지

I knew it / It's obvious

'뻔하지'는 어떤 일의 결과나 상태 따위가 훤하게 들여다보이듯이 분명하다는 뜻을 가진 표현입니다. 예상 가능하거나 자명한 상황을 나타낼 때 쓰이며, 놀랍지 않은 일에 가볍게 반응할 때도 자주 사용합니다. 때로는 더 이상 기대가 없거나 결과가 뻔하다는 의미로 비난이나 실망을 드러내는 데 쓰이기도 합니다. 억양과 상황에 따라 장난스러운 동의, 무심한 반응, 냉소적인 비판 등 다양한 뉘앙스를 전달할 수 있습니다. 변형 표현으로는 '뻔한 거 아니야?', '뻔한 이야기야.', '뻔한 레퍼토리야.' 등이 있습니다.

36 장난 아니야

No joke / Seriously

'장난 아니야'는 어떤 대상이 수준이 보통을 훨씬 넘어서는 정도로 대단하다는 뜻을 가진 표현입니다. 이 말은 맥락과 억양에 따라 여러 뉘앙스를 담을 수 있는데, 인상적이거나 훌륭한 일에 대한 놀라움과 감탄을 드러낼 때, 어떤 현상이나 상황이 매우 두드러짐을 강조할 때, 위험하거나 불편한 상황의 심각성을 표현할 때 사용됩니다. 따라서 긍정적인 의미와 부정적인 의미 모두 전달할 수 있으며, 일상 대화에서 강한 인상을 주는 반응으로 자주 활용됩니다. 비슷한 표현으로는 '진짜 대박이야', '장난 아닌데' 등이 있습니다.

37 뭐 하자는 거야?

What are you trying to do?

'뭐 하자는 거야?'는 상대방이 도전적이거나 적대적인 태도를 보인다고 느껴질 때, 또는 말과 행동이 상황에 맞지 않아 갈등이나 논쟁이 생길 때 사용하는 표현입니다. 주로 불만, 항의, 경고의 의미를 담고 있으며, 억양에 따라 강하게 따지는 느낌부터 짜증 섞인 반응까지 다양하게 전달됩니다. 비슷한 의미의 표현으로는 '왜 이래?', '무슨 의도야?' 등이 있습니다. 참고로, '뭐 하는 거야?'는 상대방이 상식 밖의 행동을 하거나 이해하기 어려운 일을 할 때 주로 사용되며, '뭐 하자는 거야?'는 나에게 도전적·적대적인 태도를 보인다고 느껴질 때 더 자주 쓰입니다.

38 그만해

That's enough / Stop it

'그만해'는 '그만하다'의 명령형 표현으로, 하던 일을 그만 멈추라는 뜻을 가지고 있습니다. 누군가에게 행동을 멈추라고 말하는 직접적인 방식으로, 주로 불쾌하거나 부적절한 행동을 멈추라고 할 때 사용됩니다. 비공식적인 상황에서 불편함, 짜증, 혹은 진지한 경고를 표현할 때 자주 쓰입니다. 유사한 표현으로는 '그만둬', '멈춰' 등이 있습니다.

39 당장

Right away / Immediately

'당장'은 '지체 없이 바로'라는 뜻을 가진 부사입니다. 즉각적인 행동을 요구할 때 쓰이며, 긴급함이나 시급성을 강조하는 상황에서 자주 사용됩니다. 특히 명령이나 지시에서 강한 어조로 재촉할 때 많이 쓰이며, 맥락에 따라 재촉, 경고, 다급함 등 다양한 뉘앙스를 전달할 수 있습니다. 유사한 표현으로는 '지금 바로', '즉시' 등이 있습니다.

40 왜 그래?

What's the matter with you?

'왜 그래?'는 '이유나 원인을 묻는 말'이라는 뜻을 가진 표현입니다. 누군가의 행동이 이상하거나, 예상 밖일 때, 또는 걱정될 때 그 이유를 묻는 데 사용됩니다. 주로 비격식적인 상황에서 상대방의 태도나 행동에 대해 질문하는 용도로 쓰이며, 말투와 억양에 따라 당황, 불만, 걱정 등 다양한 감정을 전달할 수 있습니다. 유사한 표현으로는 '왜 이래?', '무슨 일이야?' 등이 있습니다.

41 이게 뭐야?

What's this?

'이게 뭐야?'는 어떤 것이 무엇인지 묻는 표현입니다. 어떤 것에 대해 호기심, 놀람, 또는 불만을 나타낼 때 사용됩니다. 이미 벌어진 상황이 마음에 들지 않을 때 그에 대한 불만을 표현하는 용도로 쓰이기도 합니다. 예상치 못한 일이 발생했거나 무엇인지 확실하지 않을 때도 자주 사용됩니다. 유사한 표현으로는 '이게 도대체 뭐야?', '뭐지?' 등이 있습니다.

42 됐어

It's fine / Forget it

'됐어'는 '그만두거나 더 이상 필요하지 않음'을 나타내는 말입니다. 더 이상 관심이 없음을 표현하거나, 어떤 일이나 상황에 대해 포기할 때 사용됩니다. 무시하거나 거절하는 톤으로 간단히 말할 때도 쓰입니다. 말투와 억양에 따라 부드러운 거절에서 냉담한 단절까지 다양한 뉘앙스를 전달할 수 있습니다. 유사한 표현으로는 '이제 됐어', '그만 얘기해' 등이 있습니다.

43 알았어

Okay / I got it

'알았어'는 '이해하거나 인지했음을 나타내는 말'입니다. 상대방의 말이나 요청에 대한 이해와 동의를 표현할 때 사용됩니다. 이해했음을 확인시키기 위해 캐주얼하게 쓰이며, 일상 대화에서 가장 빈번하게 쓰이는 응답 중 하나입니다. 충분히 이해했다는 뜻을 여러 번 전했음에도 불구하고 상대방이 계속 확인하거나 강조할 경우, '알겠다고!'처럼 말투를 강하게 하여 답할 수도 있습니다. 유사한 표현으로는 '응, 알았어.', '이해했어.' 등이 있습니다.

44 너무해(요)

That is too much/so mean/unfair

'너무해'는 '정도가 지나치다'라는 뜻을 가진 표현입니다. 가벼운 불평이나 장난스러운 상황에서 쓰일 수 있으며, 누군가의 행동이나 말이 불공평하다고 느껴질 때, 또는 그 정도가 과하다고 판단될 때 사용됩니다. 말투와 억양에 따라 귀여운 투정부터 진지한 비난까지 다양한 감정을 전달할 수 있습니다. 유사한 표현으로는 '진짜 너무해.', '너무 심해.' 등이 있습니다.

45 신경 쓰지 마

Don't worry about it

'신경 쓰지 마' 는 사소한 데까지 세심하게 살필 필요가 없다는 뜻을 가진 표현입니다. 상대방에게 걱정하지 말라고 하거나, 어떤 일에 너무 마음을 쓰지 않도록 할 때 사용합니다. 주로 친근하거나 비격식적 대화에서 쓰이며, 상황에 따라 위로, 배려의 의미를 담을 수 있습니다. 유사한 표현으로는 '걱정하지 마.', '별거 아니야.' 등이 있습니다.

46 -지 뭐

Happens though

'-지 뭐'는 상황을 대수롭지 않게 받아들이거나 체념하듯 정리할 때 쓰이는 표현으로, 맥락과 어조에 따라 다양한 의미를 가질 수 있습니다. 예를 들어 아쉬움은 있지만 문제 삼지 않고 수용할 때, 상대방을 위로하거나 격려할 때, 이미 예측된 상황을 담담히 받아들일 때, 일이 잘 풀리지 않아 안타까움을 드러낼 때 자연스럽게 쓰입니다. 주어·시제·높임에 따라 제약이 있는데, 1·3인칭 주어일 때는 대체로 체념과 수용의 의미로, 2인칭 주어일 때는 제안이나 권유·명령의 뉘앙스로만 쓰입니다. 높임 표현에서는 '-시-'와 결합하면 어색하거나 조롱처럼 들리며, '하시지요 뭐.'처럼 쓰일 때는 높임보다는 놀람이나 의외의 의미가 강조됩니다.

47 대충

Roughly / More or less

'대충'은 '세밀하지 않고 대강 하는 것'을 뜻하는 표현입니다. 시간이 부족하거나 귀찮아서 완벽한 결과보다 빠르게 끝내려는 의도로 처리할 때, 세부적인 부분에 신경 쓰지 않고 대략적으로 하거나 추정할 때, 또는 즉흥적으로 급하게 처리할 때 사용합니다. 유사한 표현으로는 '어림잡아', '대강' 등이 있습니다.

48 나도 그래

Same here / Me too

'나도 그래'는 '나 또한 그렇다'는 뜻의 표현입니다. 누군가와 동의하거나 같은 감정을 느낄 때, 대화 중에 상대방과 같은 의견이나 감정을 공유할 때 사용합니다. 짧게 줄여서 '나도.'라고만 말하기도 하며, 주로 친근하고 비격식적인 대화에서 쓰입니다.

49 그냥

Just... / Simply...

'그냥'은 '특별한 이유나 목적 없이'라는 뜻의 표현입니다. 어떤 일을 간단히 또는 자연스럽게 설명할 때, 특별한 이유 없이 행동했음을 나타낼 때, 이유 제시를 피하거나 빠르게 거절하려 할 때 사용합니다. 특히 거절 뒤에 이어져 최소한의 이유만 암시하며 (예: '됐어. 그냥 집에서 쉴래.'), 추가적인 추궁을 완곡하게 차단하고 거리를 두는 완충 기능을 합니다. 예를 들어 '그냥 싫어.', '그냥 됐어.' 등으로 쓰입니다.

50 느낌이 이상해

Something feels off

'느낌이 이상해'는 몸의 감각이나 마음으로 깨달아 아는 기운이나 감정이 정상적이지 않다는 뜻을 가진 표현입니다. 일상적인 상황에서 분위기나 태도 등에서 미묘한 불편함이나 위화감을 느낄 때 사용됩니다. 또한 위험하거나 좋지 않은 일이 생길 것 같은 불안감이나 경계심을 나타낼 때도 쓰입니다. 말투와 억양에 따라 단순한 의아함부터 강한 경고까지 다양한 뉘앙스를 전달할 수 있습니다. 비슷한 표현으로는 '뭔가 이상해.', '분위기가 묘해.', '느낌이 싸해.' 등이 있습니다. 특히 '뭔가'와 자주 결합해 쓰이는데, '뭔가'는 '무엇인가'의 줄임말로 특정하지 못한 대상을 지칭하거나 정확히 알 수 없지만 어떤 상태를 표현할 때 사용됩니다. 따라서 '뭔가 느낌이 이상해.'라고 하면, 그 불안이나 위화감의 원인을 정확히 짚을 수는 없지만 감각적으로 어색함을 느낀다는 의미가 됩니다.

Part 2 말 습관 문형

Speech Patterns

51 같은데

I think / It seems like...

'같은데'는 형용사 '같다'에 연결 어미 '-(으)ㄴ데'가 결합한 형태로 화자의 의견, 추측, 인상이나 기억을 부드럽게 전달할 때 쓰입니다. 여기서 '-데'는 이미 제시한 판단·상황 뒤에 이어질 말이나 대비되는 내용을 암시하며 문장을 완곡하게 만드는 기능을 합니다. 이 때문에 '같은데'는 단정적인 어조를 피하고, 조심스러운 추측, 불확실한 기억, 혹은 대화를 자연스럽게 이어가기 위한 정보 전달에 자주 쓰입니다. 비슷한 의미로는 '-(으)ㄹ 것 같다' (중립적 추측), '-나 보다, -(으)ㄴ 가보다' (구어체 추측), '-(으)ㄹ 듯하다, -(으)ㄹ 법하다' (격식체 추측) 등이 있습니다. 예를 들어, '문 닫을 시간인 것 같은데'는 문을 닫을 시간일 가능성을 부드럽게 제시하며, 뒤에 이어질 설명이나 제안을 자연스럽게 예고합니다.

52 -(으)ㄹ 걸?

I guess... / Probably...

'-(으)ㄹ 걸?'은 무엇인가에 대해 추측하거나 예상할 때 친근한 사이에서 사용하는 표현입니다. 화자의 추측이 상대방의 예상이나 알고 있는 사실과 다름을 나타내며, 가벼운 반박이나 감탄의 의미를 담을 수 있습니다. 또한, 어원적으로 '-걸 그랬다'에서 '그랬다'가 생략된 형태이기 때문에, 상황에 따라 하지 않은 일이나 지나간 상황에 대한 가벼운 후회나 아쉬움을 표현하기도 합니다. 미래형 어미 '-(으)ㄹ'을 사용하여 불확실성을 나타내고, '걸'을 결합하여 대화체의 톤을 더하며, 말할 때 문장 끝의 억양을 약간 올립니다. 비슷한 표현으로는 '-겠지'가 있는데, 이는 좀 더 강한 추측을 나타내며, '-나 봐'는 보다 자연스럽고 일상적인 추정을 나타냅니다.

53 -길래

As... / Because...

'-길래'는 어떤 상황이나 감각을 직접 보고 듣고 느낀 '개인적 근거'를 바탕으로 이유를 설명할 때 쓰는 구어체 표현입니다. 문법적으로는 '-기에'의 구어형이지만, 더 주관적이고 경험적인 뉘앙스가 강해 자연스러운 일상 회화에서 빈번하게 사용됩니다. '-아/어서'가 비교적 객관적인 이유를 말하는 데 비해, '-길래'는 상황을 보고 판단해서 행동했다는 느낌이 더 드러납니다. 동사나 형용사의 어간에 붙여 사용하며, '이다'의 어간, 용언의 어간 또는 어미 '-으시-', '-었-' 뒤에 붙어 일반적인 대화에서 친밀한 관계에서 많이 쓰입니다.

54 -(으)ㄴ/는 거 아니야/아니에요?

Isn't this...? / Aren't you...?

'-(으)ㄴ/는 거 아니야?'는 무언가 사실일 가능성을 제기하거나 확인을 요청할 때 사용하는 구어체 표현입니다. 상대방이 무엇을 놓쳤는지 부드럽게 지적하거나 의심을 표현할 때 자주 사용됩니다. 예를 들어 '이거 네가 한 거 아니야?'는 단순히 사실을 확인하려는 질문일 수도 있지만, 때로는 상대방의 행동이나 말에 가볍게 도전하거나 장난스럽게 추궁하는 뉘앙스로도 쓰입니다. 예를 들어, 교실에서 책상이 엉망으로 어질러져 있는 것을 발견한 학생이, 옆 친구를 보며 장난스럽게 웃으면서 '이거 네가 한 거 아니야?'라고 말하는 장면을 떠올릴 수 있습니다. 이런 경우, 말투와 표정에 따라 가벼운 농담, 친근한 의심, 혹은 장난스러운 비난의 의미가 담기게 됩니다. 경어는 '-(으)ㄴ/는 거 아니에요?'입니다.

55 -더라고(요)

I noticed/realized...

'-더라고(요)'는 화자가 과거에 직접 경험하거나 목격하거나 깨달은 사실을 회상하며 전달할 때 사용됩니다. 예를 들어, '어제 정말 춥더라고.'처럼 개인적인 경험이나 관찰에 의한 깨달음을 전달합니다. 보통 말하는 사람이 보거나 들은 것에 대해 주관적인 경험을 기반으로 일화를 말할 때 사용하기에 주어가 1인칭인 경우에는 사용하지 않지만, 감정이나 기분, 마음 상태를 나타낼 때는 1인칭 주어로 사용되기도 합니다. 비슷한 표현으로는 '-더군(요)'와 '-더라'가 있습니다.

56 -게 됐어

I ended up... / It turned out...

'-게 됐어'는 화자의 의도와 상관없이 외부적 상황이나 흐름에 따라 어떤 일이 일어났음을 나타냅니다. 어조에 따라 원하지 않는 일이 벌어진 뉘앙스를 줄 수 있으며, 부드럽게 상황을 전달할 때 자주 사용됩니다. 또한, 시간이 지나면서 생긴 습관이나 취향 변화처럼 결과적으로 상태가 달라진 경우에도 쓰입니다. 이 외에도, 예상하지 못했지만 좋은 방향으로 일이 진행된 경우에도 사용되어, 긍정적인 결과를 자연스럽게 표현할 수 있습니다.

57 -잖아(요)

(I told you/You told me...) right?

'-잖아(요)'는 상대방이 이미 알고 있는 사실을 상기시키거나 요점을 강조할 때 사용됩니다. 예를 들어, '오늘 쉬는 날이잖아.'처럼 이미 공유된 정보를 다시 확인하거나 강조하는 경우에 쓰입니다. 또한 미리 경고했음에도 상대방이 듣지 않아 부정적인 결과가 생겼을 때, 이를 지적하거나 핀잔을 줄 때 자주 사용됩니다. '-고 있다'와 결합하면 현재 행동이 진행 중임을 강조하며, 상황을 정정하거나 답답함·불만을 표현하는 기능을 가집니다. 예를 들어, '지금 보고 있잖아.'는 이미 TV를 보고 있는 상태임을 강조하고, '지금 준비하고 있잖아.'는 이미 행동에 착수했음을 상기시키는 표현입니다. 일상 대화에서는 설득·설명·불만 표현 등 다양한 맥락에서 폭넓게 쓰입니다.

58 -고 말았어

I end(ed) up...

'-고 말았어'는 화자의 의도나 의지와 상관없이 어떤 일이 일어났음을 나타내며, 종종 후회, 좌절, 체념의 감정을 표현합니다. 이 표현은 행동의 최종성을 강조하며, 예상치 못한 결과가 발생했거나 원하지 않는 일이 벌어졌음을 나타냅니다. 주로 '결국', '끝내', '마침내'와 함께 쓰여 결과를 강조합니다. 하지만 '우리 팀이 계속 지다가 결국 이기고 말았어.'와 같이 상황이나 어조에 따라 일이 이루어지기 힘든 상황에서 힘들게 이루어 냈다는 의미를 표현할 때도 사용될 수 있습니다. 어떤 일을 이루려는 주어의 강력한 의지를 나타낼 때에는 의지를 나타내는 '-겠-'을 붙여 '-고 말겠어'와 같이 쓰이는 경우가 많습니다. 동사에 붙어 과거형으로 사용되며, 형용사와는 결합하지 않습니다. '여자 친구와 헤어지고 말았어요.'나 '여자 친구가 저를 떠나고 말았어요.'와 같이 1인칭이나 3인칭 모두에 붙어 활용될 수 있습니다. '-고' 뒤에 '야'를 붙여 강조의 의미를 더할 수 있습니다. 예컨대 '기차가 떠나 버리고야 말았다.' 등의 표현이 있습니다.

59 -는 중이야

I'm in the middle of... / On the way...

'-는 중이야'는 어떤 일을 현재 진행하고 있음을 나타내는 표현입니다. 예를 들어, '지금 숙제하는 중이야'처럼 사용됩니다. 이 표현은 현재 진행 중인 행동을 강조하며, 주로 일상 대화에서 사용됩니다. 또한 상대방이 특정 일의 진척 상황을 확인하고자 할 때 답변으로 사용될 수도 있습니다. 예컨대 '-는 어떻게 됐어?', '-는 어떻게 되어가고 있어?'라는 질문을 받았을 때 '-는 중이야'라고 대답한다면 아직 일이 완전히 마무리되지 않았지만 큰 문제 없이 일이 처리되고 있음을 암시하는 답변이 될 수 있습니다. 경어로는 '-는 중이에요' 혹은 '-는 중입니다'로 활용될 수 있습니다.

60 -나 봐

I guess... / It seems like...

'-나 봐'는 관찰이나 주변 상황, 또는 어떤 단서를 근거로 화자가 추측을 표현할 때 사용하는 구어체 표현입니다. 주로 동사나 서술격 조사 뒤에 붙어 현재나 과거의 행동·상황을 짐작할 때 쓰입니다. 형용사 뒤에서는 '-ㄴ가 봐' 형태로 변해 현재의 상태를 추측하며, 과거 상황이나 상태를 짐작할 때는 '-았/었나 봐'를 사용합니다. 예를 들어 '그 사람이 바쁜가 봐.'는 현재 상태에 대한 추측, '어제 비가 왔나 봐.'는 과거 상황에 대한 추측을 나타냅니다. 이 표현은 화자의 판단을 부드럽게 전달하는 특징이 있으며, 일상 대화에서 자주 쓰입니다. 끝을 올려 질문처럼 쓸 수도 있고, 공손하게는 '-나 봐요'나 '-나 봅니다'로 말합니다.

61 -(으)ㄹ래?

Do you want to…?

'-(으)ㄹ래?'는 'ㄹ'을 제외한 받침 있는 동사 어간 뒤에 붙어 장차 어떤 일을 하려고 하는 화자의 의사를 나타내거나, 상대방의 의향·선호를 묻는 데 쓰이는 종결 어미입니다. 자신의 의사를 간접적으로 표현하거나 친근한 사이에서 어떤 활동이나 계획을 제안할 때 자주 쓰이며, 강요하기보다 선택권을 주는 부드러운 어감을 가집니다. 정중하게는 '-(으)ㄹ래요?'로 사용할 수 있습니다.

62 -(으)ㄴ/는 것 같아

It seems like… / I think…

'-(으)ㄴ/는 것 같아'는 화자의 의견, 추측, 인상이나 기억을 부드럽게 전달할 때 쓰입니다. 현재나 미래 상황에는 '-(으)ㄴ/는 것 같아'를, 과거의 상황이나 경험을 회상할 때는 '-았/었던 것 같아'를 사용합니다. 단정적으로 말하기보다 가능성을 열어 두는 뉘앙스를 주기 때문에 '그건 좀 어려울 것 같아.', '시간이 안 될 것 같아.'처럼 부탁이나 요청을 완곡하게 거절할 때, 조심스러운 추측을 할 때, 또는 불확실한 기억을 표현할 때 자주 쓰입니다. 과거형에서는 단순한 기억뿐 아니라 여러 행동이나 상태를 묶어 과거를 생생하게 떠올리는 효과도 있습니다. 예를 들어, '그때 정말 행복했던 것 같아.'는 당시의 인상과 감정을 되살려 말하는 표현입니다.

63 -게

So that…

'-게'는 행동의 목적이나 의도를 나타낼 때 사용됩니다. 동사 어간에 '-게'를 붙여, 어떤 행동을 하는 이유나 목표를 설명합니다. 예를 들어, '사람들한테 잘 보이게 문 옆에 붙이자.'에서는 간판을 문 옆에 붙이는 이유가 '사람들에게 잘 보이도록 하기 위해서'임을 나타냅니다. 또 '사람들이 이야기할 수 있게'에서는 음악을 줄이는 목적이 '사람들이 대화할 수 있도록 하기 위해서'임을 보여 줍니다. 이렇게 '-게'는 문장의 중간에 목적절로 쓰이기도 하고, 문장 끝에 와서 이유나 목표를 강조하기도 합니다.

64 -(으)ㄹ 뻔했어

I almost (didn't, couldn't, etc)…

'-(으)ㄹ 뻔했어'는 지금까지의 상황을 볼 때 앞으로 일어날 일이 분명하게 예상되었지만, 실제로는 발생하지 않았을 때 사용합니다. 예를 들어 '넘어질 뻔했어'는 거의 넘어질 위기를 겪었지만 결국 넘어지지 않았음을 뜻합니다. 예상치 못한 일이나 위험한 순간에서 가까스로 벗어났을 때 자주 쓰이며, 놀람이나 안도의 뉘앙스를 함께 전달합니다. 또한 '간 떨어질 뻔하다'라는 관용 표현이 있는데, 이는 깜짝 놀라거나 아찔한 순간을 겪었을 때 쓰이며, 실제로 간이 떨어지는 것이 아니라 그만큼 놀랐다는 과장된 표현입니다.

65 -(으)ㄹ 테니까

So… / Since…

'-(으)ㄹ 테니까'는 화자의 의도, 추측 또는 조언을 나타내며, 앞 절이 뒤 절의 이유나 근거가 됩니다. '테 (터 + 이)'는 화자의 강한 의도나 확신을, '-니까'는 이유를 나타냅니다. 예를 들어, '내가 도울 테니까 걱정하지 마.'는 '내가 도울 것이니까 걱정하지 말라'는 의미를 전달하며, 주로 상대를 안심시키거나 계획을 제안하고 설명할 때 사용됩니다. 문법적으로 동사 어간이 모음으로 끝나면 '-ㄹ', 자음으로 끝나면 '-을'을 붙이고, '테니까'를 더합니다.

66 -(으)ㄹ지도 몰라

It might be… / I don't know, maybe…

'-(으)ㄹ지도 몰라'는 어떤 일이 일어날 가능성이 있지만 확실하지 않을 때 사용하며, 화자가 불확실성을 인정하면서도 그 가능성을 열어 두는 표현입니다. 단정적인 말투를 피하고 부드럽게 전달하는 데 효과적입니다. 동사·형용사 어간 뒤에는 미래형 '-(으)ㄹ'과 결합해 '갈지도 몰라', '추울지도 몰라'처럼 쓰입니다. 명사와 결합할 때는 서술격 조사 '이다'의 미래형을 사용해 '학생일지도 몰라'처럼 표현합니다. 주로 현재나 미래의 가능성을 나타내지만, 과거 시제와 결합해 '왔을지도 몰라'처럼 과거 상황에 대한 추측에도 쓸 수 있습니다.

67 -기만 하면

Whenever… / As long as…

'-기만 하면'은 조건을 나타낼 때 사용되며, 특히 여러 조건 중에서 결과에 결정적인 영향을 주는 유일한 조건을 강조할 때 쓰입니다. 예를 들어 '시간을 맞추기만 하면 돼.'는 '시간을 맞추는 것으로 충분하다'는 의미입니다. 또한 어떤 조건이 충족되면 항상 같은 결과가 반복적으로 발생함을 강조할 때도 사용됩니다. 예를 들어 '두 사람은 만나기만 하면 싸워'는 '만나는 상황이 되면 반드시 싸움이 벌어진다'는 뜻을 담고 있습니다.

68 -았/었으면 좋겠어

I wish… / I just hope…

'-았/었으면 좋겠어'는 현재와 다른 상태나 상황을 바라는 마음을 나타내며, 실제 과거를 묘사하는 것이 아니라 이루어지지 않았거나 아직 이루어지지 않은 일에 대한 희망이나 상상을 표현합니다. 예를 들어, '날씨가 조금 더 따뜻했으면 좋겠어.'는 지금은 날씨가 춥지만 따뜻해지기를 바란다는 뜻입니다. 또한 '그때 조금만 더 열심히 했으면 좋았을걸.'처럼 과거 상황에 대한 후회나 아쉬움을 나타낼 수도 있습니다. 이 표현은 단순한 희망뿐 아니라, 상황이 달랐다면 가능했을 일에 대한 상상이나 안타까움을 드러낼 때도 사용됩니다.

69 -(으)ㄹ 거야

I'll make sure… / I'm going to…

'-(으)ㄹ 거야'는 화자의 미래 의도나 결정을 표현하거나, 아직 일어나지 않은 일에 대한 강한 추측을 나타낼 때 사용됩니다. 예를 들어, 친구와 저녁 약속 후 집에 가려고 할 때 '이제 집에 갈 거야.'라고 하면, 이는 집에 가겠다는 화자의 계획과 결심을 드러냅니다. 또, 운동회에서 경기를 지켜보며 '아마 1반이 우승할 거야.'라고 말하면, 실제 결과를 아직 알 수 없더라도 화자가 1반의 우승을 확신하고 있음을 보여 줍니다. 이 표현은 비격식적이며 주로 일상 대화에서 쓰입니다.

70 -았/었더라면

If I had…

'-았/었더라면'은 과거에 일어나지 않은 가정 상황에 대해 이야기할 때 사용되며, 종종 후회나 다른 결과를 상상하는 의미를 전달합니다. 예를 들어, '그때 공부했더라면 좋았을 텐데.'는 과거에 공부하지 않은 것에 대한 아쉬움과, 공부했더라면 더 좋은 결과가 있었을 것을 표현합니다. 이 표현은 주로 뒤 절에 '좋았을 텐데'처럼 바람·후회를 나타내는 문장이 이어집니다.

71 -지 않을까?

Don't you think…? / Maybe it will…

'-지 않을까?'는 어떤 일이 일어날 가능성을 조심스럽게 추측하거나, 자신의 생각에 대해 상대방의 동의를 구할 때 사용합니다. 예를 들어 '그 사람이 오지 않을까?'는 '그 사람이 올 가능성이 있다'는 추측을 하면서도, 단정적으로 말하지 않고 부드럽게 의견을 제시하는 표현입니다. 긍정형 '-(으)ㄹ까?'가 가능성이나 의도를 직접적으로 묻는 데 비해, '-지 않을까?'는 부정형을 사용하여 실제로는 긍정적인 가능성에 무게를 두면서도 완곡하게 말하는 뉘앙스를 가집니다.

72 -고 나서

Then… / After…

'-고 나서'는 하나의 행동이 완료된 후에 다른 행동이 일어나는 것을 나타낼 때 사용합니다. 받침 유무와 관계없이 동사 어간 뒤에 '-고 나서'를 붙여 쓰며, 첫 번째 행동의 완료를 강조합니다. 예를 들어, '밥 먹고 나서 영화를 보자.'는 밥을 다 먹은 뒤에 영화를 보자는 뜻을 나타냅니다. '밥 먹고 영화를 보자.'와 의미는 비슷하지만, '나서'를 덧붙이면 첫 번째 행동이 끝난 시점을 더 분명히 합니다. 주로 사건의 순서를 설명하거나 계획을 제안할 때 사용됩니다.

73 -다가

While…

'-다가'는 하나의 행동이 진행되는 중에 다른 행동이나 사건이 갑자기 끼어드는 상황을 나타낼 때 사용됩니다. 주로 예상치 못한 상황을 묘사할 때 쓰이며, 동사 어간에 바로 붙여 사용합니다. 예를 들어, '집에 가다가 친구를 만났어.'는 집에 가는 도중에 우연히 친구를 만난 상황을 나타냅니다. 또한 '공부하다가 잠이 들었어.'처럼 진행 중이던 행동이 멈추고 다른 상황으로 전환되는 경우, 즉 주로 사건의 순서를 묘사하는 서술에서 자주 사용됩니다.

74 -(으)ㄹ 만해

It's worth doing…

'-(으)ㄹ 만해'는 어떤 행동을 할 타당한 이유가 있을 정도로 가치가 있거나, 그 행동이 가능함을 나타낼 때 사용합니다. 예를 들어, '이 영화는 볼 만해'는 이 영화가 볼 가치가 있다는 의미이고, '그는 차를 살 만한 형편이 못 된다.'는 차를 살 수 있는 경제적 여건이 안 된다는 뜻입니다. 동사 어간이 모음으로 끝나면 '-ㄹ 만해', 자음으로 끝나면 '-을 만해'를 붙여 사용합니다. 주로 활동, 경험, 물건, 장소 등이 충분히 시도하거나 경험할 가치가 있음을 추천하거나 평가하는 상황에서 쓰입니다.

75 -자마자

As soon as…

'-자마자'는 앞의 행동이 끝나자마자 바로 다음 행동이 이어지는 상황을 나타냅니다. 예를 들어, '집에 가자마자 친구를 만났어.'는 '집에 도착한 순간, 바로 친구를 만난' 상황을 표현합니다. 또한, '공부하다가 잠들었어.'와 같이 진행 중인 행동이 갑작스럽게 멈추거나 다른 상황으로 전환되는 맥락에서도 쓰입니다. 이 표현은 주로 이야기의 흐름에서 행동의 빠른 순서를 강조할 때 자주 사용됩니다.

76 -(으)ㄴ/는 편이야

Tend to be…

'-(으)ㄴ/는 편이야'는 화자가 특정 경향, 성향, 혹은 비교적 일관된 특성을 가지고 있음을 표현하는 말입니다. 과장하거나 절대적으로 단정 짓기보다, 대체로 그렇다는 뉘앙스를 주어 진술을 부드럽게 만듭니다. 동작 동사의 현재 경향에는 '-는 편이야'를, 과거 경험에는 '-(으)ㄴ 편이야'를, 형용사나 상태 서술에는 '-(으)ㄴ 편이야'를 사용합니다. 예를 들어, '나는 야채를 자주 먹는 편이야.'는 '야채를 비교적 자주 먹는 경향이 있다'는 의미이며, '그 사람은 말이 적은 편이야.'는 '평소에 말이 적은 성향이 있다'는 뜻입니다.

77 -(으)ㄴ/는 척하다

To pretend…

'-(으)ㄴ/는 척하다'는 실제로는 그렇지 않지만, 마치 그런 것처럼 거짓으로 꾸미거나 행동하는 것을 나타내는 표현입니다. 서술어 어간이 자음으로 끝나면 '-은 척하다', 모음으로 끝나면 '-ㄴ 척하다'를 씁니다. 동작 동사에는 주로 과거형 '-(으)ㄴ/는'을 사용하여, 실제로는 일어나지 않은 행동을 한 것처럼 가장하는 의미를 줍니다. 예를 들어, '못 들은 척했어.'는 실제로 들었지만 들은 사실을 숨기기 위해 들리지 않은 것처럼 행동했음을 나타냅니다.

78 -(으)ㄹ 리가 없어

There's no way…

'-(으)ㄹ 리가 없어'는 '리'가 이유나 근거를 나타내는 의존 명사이므로, 어떤 일에 대한 이유나 근거가 전혀 없음을 강조하여 그 일이 불가능하거나 사실이 아님을 확신하거나 의심할 때 사용합니다. 예를 들어, '그 사람이 나를 좋아할 리가 없어.'는 그 가능성을 강하게 부정하는 표현이며, 대화 중 상황에 대한 의구심이나 불신을 나타낼 때 자주 쓰입니다.

79 -(으)ㄴ 적 있어?

Have you ever…

'-(으)ㄴ 적 있다/없다'는 어떤 일을 과거에 경험한 사실이 있는지 없는지를 나타내는 표현입니다. 주로 '…한 적 있어?'처럼 질문형으로 쓰여 상대방의 경험을 물을 때 사용하며, 대답을 할 때는 긍정형 '…한 적 있다', 부정형 '…한 적 없다'를 사용할 수 있습니다. 서술어가 동작 동사일 경우 동사 어간 뒤에 '-ㄴ'을 붙이고, 서술 동사는 '-은'을 붙입니다. 이 표현은 경험을 공유하거나 비교할 때도 자주 쓰입니다.

80 -는 게 낫지 않아?

Isn't it better…?

'-는 게 낫지 않아?'는 더 나은 행동이나 선택을 제안하거나, 대안이 더 좋지 않겠느냐고 물을 때 사용합니다. 동작 동사 어간에 '-는'을 붙이고, '-게 낫다'를 덧붙여 사용합니다. 주로 친근한 조언이나 제안을 할 때 쓰이며, 앞에 '보다'를 붙여 두 가지 선택지를 비교하거나, 부사 '차라리'와 함께 사용되는 경우가 많습니다. 구어체에서는

'보다는'이 '보단'으로 줄어드는 일이 흔합니다. 예를 들어, '늦게 가는 것보단 지금 가는 게 낫지 않아?'는 화자가 지금 가는 것이 더 좋은 선택이라고 생각함을 나타냅니다.

81 -기도 하고…

Also… / Both… and…

'-기도 하고'는 하나의 대상이나 상황에 대해 두 가지 이상의 성질, 행동, 특징을 나열할 때 사용합니다. 같은 문장 안에서 긍정적인 성질끼리, 부정적인 성질끼리, 또는 서로 다른 성질을 함께 표현할 수 있습니다. 동사나 형용사 어간에 '-기도 하다'를 붙여 사용하며, 반복적으로 사용하여 병렬 구조를 만드는 경우가 많습니다. 예를 들어, '그 영화는 재밌기도 하고 슬프기도 해.'는 그 영화가 재미와 슬픔을 동시에 전달한다는 의미입니다. 이 표현은 감정, 성격, 상태, 행동 등을 함께 묘사할 때 자주 쓰입니다.

82 -(으)ㄹ 수밖에 없어

Can't help… / It's inevitable…

'-(으)ㄹ 수밖에 없어'는 다른 방법이나 선택이 전혀 없어서 어떤 일을 반드시 하게 되는 상황을 나타냅니다. 동사 어간에 '-(으)ㄹ 수밖에 없다'는 구조를 붙여 사용하며, 불가피하거나 필연적인 상황을 강조합니다. 예를 들어, '그 말을 믿을 수밖에 없어.'는 그 말을 믿는 것 외에는 다른 방법이 없음을 의미합니다. 이 표현은 말하는 사람이 상황을 바꿀 수 없는 무력감이나 당위성을 느낄 때 자주 쓰입니다.

83 -(으)ㄹ 필요가 없어

No need to…

'-(으)ㄹ 필요가 없어'는 어떤 행동이나 상태가 필요하지 않거나 요구되지 않는다는 뜻을 나타냅니다. 동사 어간에 모음으로 끝나면 '-ㄹ', 자음으로 끝나면 '-을'을 붙이고, '필요가 없다'를 덧붙여 사용합니다. 형용사와 결합하여 '그렇게 심각할 필요가 없어.'처럼 상태나 정도가 불필요함을 표현할 수도 있습니다. 예를 들어, '걱정할 필요가 없어.'는 걱정이 전혀 필요하지 않음을 상대방에게 안심시키는 말입니다. 이 표현은 안심, 조언, 설득 등 부정적인 감정을 완화하거나 불필요한 행동을 줄일 때 자주 쓰입니다.

84 -거든(요)

Actually…

'-거든(요)'는 이유를 설명하거나 추가적인 맥락을 제공할 때 사용되며, 청자에게 이유나 배경을 설명하거나 감탄·자랑의 뉘앙스를 전할 때, 그리고 앞으로 할 이야기를 꺼내기 위한 전제로 사용할 때 쓰입니다. 동사나 형용사 어간에 '-거든' 또는 '-거든요'를 붙여 사용하며, 말투에 따라 친근하고 부드러운 설명부터 강한 강조까지 다양한 느낌을 줄 수 있습니다.

85 -아/어도 돼?

Is it okay/fine…?

'-아/어도 되다'는 어떤 행동이 허용되는지, 또는 상대가 그렇게 행동해도 괜찮은지를 묻거나 말할 때 사용하는 표현입니다. 기본적으로 허락·용인을 나타내지만, 실제 회화에서는 단순한 허락 요청 외에도 어떤 행동의 적절성·타당성을 확인하거나 문제 삼을 때도 자주 쓰입니다. 예를 들어 '이렇게 해도 돼?'는 허락을 묻는 의미일 수도 있지만, 상황에 따라 '이 방식이 맞아?' 또는 '그렇게 해도 문제가 없겠어?'라는 방법·행동의 정당성 확인으로 쓰이기도 합니다. 또한 '저런 걸 시켜도 돼?'처럼 상대방의 행동이 도덕적·사회적으로 맞지 않는다고 생각하며 비판하거나 항의할 때도 사용됩니다. 반말로는 '-아/어도 돼?', 존댓말로는 '-아/어도 돼요?', 격식체로는 '-아/어도 됩니까?'처럼 공손도에 따라 변형됩니다. 비슷한 의미의 표현으로는 '-아/어도 괜찮다', '-아/어도 좋아요', '-아/어도 무방합니다'가 있으며, 반대 의미로는 금지와 불허를 나타내는 '-(으)면 안 되다'가 있습니다. 단순한 허락 요청뿐 아니라 '이렇게 해도 돼?'에서 처럼 방법의 적절성을 확인할 때도 쓰입니다.

86 -기 싫어

To not want to…

'-기 싫어'는 어떤 행동을 하고 싶지 않거나 꺼린다는 뜻을 나타냅니다. 동사 어간에 '-기'를 붙이고 '싫다'를 덧붙여 사용하며, 반말로는 '-기 싫어', 존댓말로는 '-기 싫어요'로 씁니다. 예를 들어, '일하기 싫어'는 일을 하고 싶지 않다는 의미입니다. 주로 감정이나 의사를 직접적으로 표현하는 구어체에서 자주 사용되며, 상황에 따라 장난스럽거나 진지한 어조로 쓰일 수 있습니다. 비슷한 표현으로는 '-고 싶지 않다'가 있으며, 이는 다소 중립적이고 완곡하게 거부 의사를 표현하는 반면, '-기 싫다'는 감정이 보다 직접적이고 강하게 전달되는 경우가 많습니다.

87 -았/었어야 했는데

Should have...

'-았/었어야 했는데'는 했어야 했지만 하지 못한 일에 대한 후회나 아쉬움을 나타냅니다. 동사 어간에 과거 시제 어미 '-았/었-'을 붙인 뒤, 당위성을 나타내는 '-아/어야 하다'를 결합하고, 상황을 배경으로 설명하거나 다음 내용을 이어 주는 '-(으)ㄴ/는데'를 덧붙여 사용합니다. 예를 들어, '일찍 출발했어야 했는데.'는 일찍 출발하지 못한 것에 대한 안타까움과 반성을 표현합니다. 이 표현은 주로 과거의 행동이나 선택을 되돌아보며 잘못이나 실수를 인정하거나 아쉬움을 전할 때 쓰입니다.

88 -더니

As a result...

'-더니'는 특정 행동이나 상태 후에 관찰된 변화나 결과를 묘사하는 데 사용되며, 동사 어간에 '-더니'를 붙여 사용합니다. 예를 들어, '많이 먹었더니 배가 아프다.'는 많이 먹은 것과 배가 아픈 결과를 연결합니다. 주로 화자 본인의 경험과 그 결과를 설명할 때는 과거형 어미 '-았/었-'을 붙여 사용하고, 타인의 상황에 대해 설명할 때는 과거형 어미 '-았/었-'없이 현재형으로 사용됩니다. 예컨대 '잘하려고 노력했더니 좋은 결과를 얻었네.'라고 말한다면 이는 본인의 행동과 그 결과에 대한 평가가 되지만, '잘하려고 노력하더니 좋은 결과를 얻었네.' 라고 말한다면 이는 타인의 행동과 그 결과에 대한 평가가 됩니다.

89 -(으)ㄴ/는가 보다, -나 보다

Looks like... / I guess...

'-(으)ㄴ/는가 보다, -나 보다'는 관찰이나 상황에 근거하여 어떤 사실을 추측할 때 사용하는 표현입니다. 형용사에는 '-(으)ㄴ/는가 보다'를, 동사에는 '-나 보다'를 붙여 사용합니다. 예를 들어, '저 사람은 바쁜가 보다.'는 상대방의 행동이나 표정을 보고 바쁘다고 추측하는 의미입니다. 이 표현은 주로 일상 대화에서 쓰이며, 단정하지 않고 부드럽게 생각을 전하는 어조를 나타냅니다. 구어체로는 '-(으)ㄴ/는가 봐, -나 봐'를 많이 사용합니다.

90 -(으)ㄹ까 봐

To be worried/afraid...

'-(으)ㄹ까 봐'는 어떤 일이 일어날 가능성에 대해 걱정하거나 두려워하는 마음을 나타냅니다. 예를 들어, '늦을까 봐 서둘렀어.'는 늦을 가능성을 걱정해 서둘렀다는 뜻입니다. 동사 어간이 자음으로 끝나면 '-을까 봐', 모음으로 끝나면 '-ㄹ까 봐'를 사용하며, 형용사와도 결합해 '추울까 봐 옷을 더 껴입었어.'처럼 상태에 대한 우려를 표현할 수 있습니다. 주로 부정적인 결과를 피하거나 대비하기 위한 행동의 이유를 설명할 때 쓰이며, '-(으)ㄹ까 봐' 뒤에 '걱정돼', '두려워' 등의 감정 표현이 오면 화자의 심리 상태를 직접적으로 드러낼 수 있습니다.

91 -기로 했어

Decided to...

'-기로 하다'는 어떤 행동이나 계획을 하기로 결정했음을 나타냅니다. 동사 어간에 '-기로'를 붙이고 뒤에 '하다'를 결합해 사용하며, 반말로는 '-기로 했어', 존댓말로는 '-기로 했어요'로 씁니다. 예를 들어, '친구랑 영화를 보기로 했어.'는 영화를 보기로 한 결정을 나타냅니다. 이 표현은 주로 숙고나 의논 끝에 내린 결정을 강조할 때 쓰이며, 미래 계획을 전달하거나 약속을 나타낼 때도 사용됩니다.

92 -는 바람에

Due to... (negative consequence)

'-는 바람에'는 예기치 못한, 주로 부정적인 결과의 이유를 설명할 때 사용됩니다. 예를 들어, '비가 오는 바람에 소풍이 취소되었어.' 는 비로 인해 소풍을 취소하게 된 이유를 나타냅니다. 이 표현은 형용사와는 함께 쓰이지 못하고 동사 어간에 붙여 사용하며, 주로 원하지 않는 결과를 초래한 상황을 강조할 때 사용됩니다. 또한, 예상 밖의 결과가 생겼을 때만 긍정적인 상황에서 쓰입니다. 이 표현은 이미 일이 난 결과에 대한 이유를 설명하기 때문에 '-는 바람에' 다음에는 항상 과거형이 옵니다. 그러므로 명령문이나 청유문과는 함께 사용할 수 없습니다.

93 (-(으)ㄴ/는) 덕분에

Thanks to…

'(-(으)ㄴ/는) 덕분에'는 긍정적인 결과나 상황이 누군가의 도움이나 영향으로 인해 발생했음을 나타내며, 감사하거나 고마운 마음을 표현할 때 사용합니다. 명사 뒤에는 '덕분에'를, 자음으로 끝나는 동사 어간 뒤에는 '-은 덕분에'를, 모음으로 끝나는 동사 어간 뒤에는 '-ㄴ 덕분에'를 씁니다. 예를 들어, '네 덕분에 시험을 잘 봤어.'는 상대방의 도움으로 시험에서 좋은 성적을 거두었음을 의미합니다. 비슷한 표현으로 '-기 때문에'는 원인을 중립적으로 설명하며, '(으)로 인해'는 공식적·격식 있는 문장에서 쓰입니다. 반면 '(-(으)ㄴ/는) 덕분에'는 긍정적인 결과를 강조하고, 감사의 뜻을 전하는 데 초점이 있습니다.

94 -(으)면 할수록

The more ..., the more...

'-(으)면 할수록'은 한 가지 일이 증가하거나 반복될수록 그와 관련된 다른 일도 함께 증가하거나 변화하는 관계를 나타냅니다. 동사 어간이 자음으로 끝나면 '-으면 할수록', 모음으로 끝나면 '-면 할수록'을 붙여 사용합니다. 예를 들어, '공부하면 할수록 실력이 늘어.'는 공부를 많이 할수록 실력이 향상된다는 의미입니다. 이 표현은 한 행동이나 조건이 더해질수록 그에 따른 결과나 상태가 점차 변한다고 설명할 때 쓰입니다.

95 -고 싶어(요)

Want to…

'-고 싶어요'는 어떤 행동이나 상태에 대한 욕구나 바람을 나타내는 표현으로, 희망이나 소망을 가장 일반적으로 표현할 때 쓰입니다. 동사 어간에 '-고 싶다'를 붙여 사용하며, 반말로는 '-고 싶어', 정중하게는 '-고 싶어요'로 말합니다. 예를 들어, '나는 여행을 가고 싶어.'는 여행을 가고 싶은 마음을 표현합니다. '싶다'는 문맥에 따라 단순한 욕구뿐 아니라, 아쉬움 ('다시 가고 싶다.'), 회상 ('그때로 돌아가고 싶다.'), 간접적인 제안 ('같이 가고 싶으시면 말씀하세요.')처럼 다양한 의미로도 활용될 수 있습니다.

96 이/가 아니라

It's not… but…

'이/가 아니라'는 어떤 것이 아니라 다른 것임을 나타내는 표현으로, 앞의 내용을 부정하고 뒤의 내용을 강조할 때 사용합니다. 자음으로 끝나는 명사 뒤에는 '이 아니라'를, 모음으로 끝나는 명사 뒤에는 '가 아니라'를 씁니다. 예를 들어, '나는 학생이 아니라 선생님이야.'는 학생임을 부정하고 선생님임을 강조합니다. 이러한 부정-대조 표현은 일상 대화뿐 아니라 공식적인 설명이나 정정 상황에서도 널리 쓰입니다.

97 -(으)려고

In order to… / Planning to…

'-(으)려고'는 동작의 목적이나 의도, 또는 곧 일어날 움직임이나 상태의 변화를 나타낼 때 사용합니다. 받침 없는 동사 어간, 'ㄹ' 받침인 동사 어간, 또는 어미 '-(으)시-' 뒤에 결합합니다. 어떤 행동을 할 계획이나 욕망을 나타낼 때는, 예를 들어 '내일은 일찍 일어나려고 한다.'처럼 의도를 표현합니다. 또한 가까운 시점에 변화나 사건이 일어날 조짐을 나타낼 때도 쓰입니다. 예를 들어 '하늘을 보니 곧 비가 쏟아지려고 한다.'는 비가 곧 내릴 것 같은 상태를 묘사합니다. 청유형이나 명령형 문장에서는 사용되지 않으며, 주로 목적·계획·의도를 전달하거나 임박한 상황을 묘사할 때 쓰입니다.

98 -아/어도

Even if… / Even though…

'-아/어도'는 어떤 조건이나 장애물이 있어도 그 일이 일어나거나 상태가 유지된다는 의미를 나타내는 연결 어미입니다. 동사뿐 아니라 형용사와도 결합해 쓰이며, 조건이나 상황을 가정하거나 양보하는 뜻을 표현합니다. 어간이 '아' 또는 '오'로 끝나면 '-아도', 그 외의 모음으로 끝나면 '-어도'를 붙입니다. 예를 들어, '피곤해도 일하고 싶어.'는 피곤하지만 일을 하고 싶은 마음이 있다는 상반된 상황을 나타내고, '비싸도 살 거예요.'는 가격이 높아도 구매하겠다는 의지를 표현합니다. 이 표현은 주로 '하지만'과 비슷한 의미로, 실제 상황뿐 아니라 가정된 상황에서도 사용됩니다.

99 -(으)ㄴ/는 대로

As soon as… / According to …

'-(으)ㄴ/는 대로'는 어떤 일이 일어난 직후 또는 그 상태 그대로 다른 일이 이어짐을 나타냅니다. 동사 어간이 과거형일 경우 모음으로 끝나면 '-ㄴ 대로', 자음으로 끝나면 '-은 대로'를 사용하며, 현재형일 경우 '-는 대로'를 붙입니다. 예를 들어, '도착하는 대로 전화해.'는 도착하는 순간 바로 전화하라는 의미이고, '말한 대로 진행했어.'는 이전에 말한 내용 그대로 실행했음을 나타냅니다. 이 표현은 한 행동이 끝나면 바로 다른 행동이 이어지거나, 기존 상태를 그대로 유지함을 강조할 때 쓰입니다. 비슷한 표현으로는 '-자마자'가 있습니다.

100 -는 동안에

While doing…

'-는 동안에'는 한 행동이 진행되는 시간에 다른 행동이 동시에 일어나거나, 어떤 상태가 지속됨을 나타낼 때 사용됩니다. 예를 들어, '내가 요리하는 동안에 상대방은 설거지해.'는 내가 요리하는 시간 동안 상대방은 설거지를 하라는 뜻입니다. 동사 어간에 '-는'을 붙여 현재 진행되는 행동을 나타낸 뒤, 그 기간을 의미하는 '동안에'를 결합해 사용합니다. 문맥에 따라 단순히 동시 진행뿐 아니라, 특정 상태나 상황이 지속되는 기간을 설명하는 데도 쓰입니다.

K-Drama 색인 Index of K-Drama

100개 말 습관 표현/문형 목록 Alphabetical Index of 100 Expressions & Patterns

ㅇ

ㅈ

ㅎ

MEMO

MEMO

MEMO

MEMO

Written by Nielbock-Yoon Jaewon
Translated by Isabel Kim Dzitac
First Published February, 2026
First Printing February, 2026
Publisher Chung Kyudo
Editor-in-Chief Lee Suk-hee
Editor Lee Hyeonsoo, Oh Jieun
Cover design Yoon Ji-young
Interior design Yoon Hyun-joo
Illustrated by Huttzza
Voice Actor Kim Sung-hee, Yu Seon-il

다락원 Published by Darakwon, Inc.
Darakwon Bldg., 211 Munbal-ro, Paju-si
Gyeonggi-do, 10881 Republic of Korea
Tel : 82-2-736-2031 Fax : 82-2-732-2037
(Marketing Dept. ext.: 250~252 Editorial Dept. ext.: 420~426)

ISBN : 978-89-277-3357-7 13710

http://www.darakwon.co.kr
http://koreanbooks.darakwon.co.kr
Visit the Darakwon homepage to learn about our other publications and promotions and to download the contents in MP3 format.